THE BEER DRINKER'S COMPANION

THE BEER DRINKER'S COMPANION

FRANK BAILLIE

DAVID & CHARLES: NEWTON ABBOT

0 7153 6201 1

© Frank Baillie 1973, 1974

Reprinted August 1974

New impression with new information on pages 291-292 April
1974

Set in 11 on 12 pt Aldine by Print Origination Liverpool
and printed in Great Britain
by Redwood Burn Ltd Trowbridge and Esher
for David & Charles (Holdings) Limited
South Devon House Newton Abbot Devon

Contents

List of Plates

Acknowledgements

Without the co-operation and help of the brewers and many members of the brewing industry this book would have been impossible to compile with any semblance of accuracy. I am indebted to the brewers for much information, the checking of facts already possessed and guidance on technical matters; to Mr. J.F. Walker BSc, FRIC, MI BIOL, FIFST, consultant zymologist of Messrs Briant & Harman (consulting and analytical chemists) for invaluable technical guidance; to Wigan Richardson & Co, hop merchants (Mr J.H. Welton), who gave useful information on hops and the hops industry; to ABM (Malting) Ltd (Mr T.A.A. Macpherson and Mr G.S. Riley), who helped on the subject of the malting process; to Cyril Pearl for permission to use a quotation in the postscript from his book (on Australian beer) *Beer, Glorious Beer!*, which is a quotation from his novel, *Pantaloons and Antics*: to Keith Osborne, researcher on brewery history, for some useful information; to all of them I raise an overflowing pint of one of the brewing industry's superb products.

Photographs were kindly supplied by Arthur Guinness Son & Co Ltd (pp34, 68), Hall & Woodhouse Ltd (p 133), Eldridge, Pope & Co Ltd (pp 33 *below,* 67, 134 *above*), Daniel Thwaites & Co Ltd (p 168 *below*). The other photographs are the author's.

Introduction

The shelves of any bookstore where books about drinks are sold are overflowing with books about wine. Wine from famous vineyards; how to drink wine; when to drink it; there is scarcely any information that the wine connoisseur is denied. But apart from a few guides to home brewing there is not very much with which the beer enthusiast can satisfy his thirst for knowledge as readily as he can his thirst for his favourite tipple. Yet in many parts of the world, beer, with its infinite variety of palate and even bouquet, is man's most popular drink.

There is a widely held illusion that all beer tastes alike. The same person is often conservative in his attitude to beer but adventurous when choosing wine or cheese for dinner, and yet emotion does run high when beer is discussed. Enthusiastic beer drinkers defend their own particular favourite to the last drop, and fierce denunciations of beer from other parts of the country are regular features of pub conversations ('not like that lousy southern stuff . . .'). The truth is that no region has a monopoly of good, strong or any other type of beer and such remarks are usually inspired by a healthy spirit of rivalry. (To set the balance right, some of the world's strongest beers are brewed in the south of England.)

Prejudices and misinformation are rife and there are many true stories to bear this out which, with variations, could be repeated up and down the country. Stories like what happened in a pub of an independent brewer in the South West. A self-styled beer expert walked into this pub with a continental friend who was evidently being initiated into the delights of drinking British beer. There was an ash tray on one of the tables which conspicuously advertised the wares of a well-known national brewer, and the 'expert' duly ordered the national brewer's famous (and heavily advertised) keg beer. On being asked for two pints the landlord. without batting an eyelid and with commendable commercial instinct, served two pints of the local brew. After downing these with much satisfaction and lip-smacking two more pints were ordered. Then the landlord was called away to attend to other matters so when it was time for the third pint an assistant was minding the bar. When asked for the famous national beer he said—with commendable honesty—that they sold only the local brew. The 'man with a prejudice' muttered something about never drinking that stuff and was through the door of that pub faster than it takes to say 'cheers'. It all goes to show that people very often do not know what they are really about to drink when ordering a pint.

With the unique choice at the disposal of the British beer-drinker—there are still over a thousand brands to be found in Britain's pubs, not including imported beers—it is a pity that there has been no guide to the brewing industry and its wares (perhaps not so needed in the past when people travelled less and there was less peril from amalgamations and standardisation). The philosophy that 'beer is beer', implying that all beer tastes alike, could not be more misguided. Surely the variety of subtle flavours that can be enjoyed is as wide as that which is made so much of by the wine connoisseur.

Nor is there much information about the beer in the pubs themselves, and in a pub belonging to an unfamiliar brewer a new customer is likely to be quite bewildered and unsure which of the many brands to order. Sometimes the complete range of a brewer's wares is not offered in every pub, so all in all a little more customer orientation would not come amiss. For instance, it would be helpful to know the gravity of the beer about to be consumed, especially when drinking and driving is not recommended (a policy which, if followed to the letter, would put the brewers and many other people out of business—and would deny the government a large slice of revenue). It would be good to be able to see at a glance whether a beer is a true draught and living beer or a keg beer, whether it is from a cask or large container (such as with tank beers), and perhaps even whether the beer is dry or sweet. Wine bottles or wine catalogues usually tell the prospective tippler whether it is dry or sweet, but the beer drinker has to find out for himself—and the price of beer in some pubs is approaching that of wine. The occasional landlord has been known to offer a sip of his draught and keg beers to a stranger before he makes the vital decision—a splendid act of public relations which should not be necessary.

As these ideals are not likely to be realised, this book has been compiled, and it is dedicated to the many beer drinkers who would like to find, know about and drink some of the wonderful beers still left to us before it is too late.

CHAPTER 1

The Language of Beer

1 WHAT IS BEER?

Very simply, beer is the result of the combination of malt (from which sugars are derived), hops, yeast and water in the right proportions and at the right temperatures. It could also be described as an extract of malted barley, boiled with hops and fermented with yeast. Beer is also called 'ale', and a briefing on English beer for American servicemen during World War II must have done little to strengthen Allied unity. It ran as follows: 'The usual English drink is beer, which is not an imitation of German beer, as our beer is, but ale (but they usually call it beer or bitter)'. The truth is that nowadays beer and ale are synonymous and both names are used to distinguish the drink from lager (and exactly what lager is, is explained later). Ale is the old English name, and the name beer did not become well-known until the late Middle Ages when hops were introduced from the Low Countries. At that time the difference between beer and ale was that beer was a hopped drink whilst ale was brewed without hops.

It all goes back many years—in fact to around 4000 BC in Mesopotamia where barley grew wild—and that the Mediterranean countries knew how to make a fermented drink from barley in those days is known from archaeological evidence. But the beer must have been very different, and although made from barley which was malted in much the same way as in modern times it was probably a thick sweet syrupy drink as honey and spices are said to have been added. It must have spread through the Middle East to Western Europe where it had become the national drink by the beginning of the Christian era. It is known that beer—and hang-overs—certainly existed in Britain at this time, but it is possible that a form of beer was drunk in Britain quite a few years before that—altogether 5,000 years ago, as there is archaeological evidence that barley was grown on these shores at that time. Authorities are of the opinion that these barleys originated from the Near East, but whether the knowledge of how to turn them into a fermented drink came at the same time is unproven.

The arrival of hops from the Continent of Europe in the fifteenth century must have been an exciting new development. Hops have very useful preservative powers as well as conferring bitterness and other subtle flavours. The permutations now available to the brewer to achieve his own preferred flavours are impressive—hops, malt (source of sugar and flavour), yeast (the brewing agent and also a very important source of flavour), water (which nowadays can be chemically adjusted to suit requirements) and sugars. Sugars provide additional fermentable material and also another means of flavour adjustment. They were first sanctioned to be used in brewing by an Act of Parliament in 1847. From the Middle Ages to the present day beer has always been a beverage remarkable for its infinite variety of palate and even bouquet—as many a home brewer has found to his cost.

The part that the different ingredients play in the brewing process will be explained more fully in the pages to come.

2   BEER TYPES DEFINED

DRAUGHT BEERS AND KEG BEERS
Draught beer has, for many years, been defined as beer dispensed from a tap and served from a cask or other container on the premises. This has become accepted by usage but nowadays is completely misleading and out of date. By this definition keg and container beers are also draught beers, yet they have quite different characters. True draught beer is a living beer which is naturally conditioned. That means matured by the natural effervescence of carbon dioxide (CO_2 or carbonic acid gas) and not by its artificial injection. Keg beers are chilled (to precipitate solids), filtered (to remove these solids, including living yeast cells—a source of flavour) and sometimes pasteurised (heated to around 140°F to kill any yeast cells remaining). Carbon dioxide gas is usually injected under pressure to give the beer a sparkle and fizz. In other words, keg beers are like bottled beers (normally with less CO_2 than bottled beers) but delivered in special sealed casks or kegs. Inevitably they have a different character from true, traditional draught beers.

When a draught beer is racked into the cask a small quantity of sugar solution (priming sugar) is sometimes added to bring about a small secondary fermentation and some dry hops may be added to the cask before filling (this may also be done with certain keg beers). The purpose of this is to give the beer a

pleasant hop aroma, an extra hop flavour, and to help
keep down any solids after fining. Fining consists of
the addition of a thick, colourless solution which has
the property of attracting yeast and sediment which
then separates out and makes the beer bright. Finings
are made from isinglass which is manufactured from
the swimming bladder of the sturgeon or certain
other fish and it does not affect the palate of the beer
in any way. Certain other materials may also be used.
When the cask is delivered to the pub the finings have
just been added (sometimes the landlord used to add
them himself) and the cask must stand for a few days
to allow the beer to clear. During the few days in the
pub's cellar before it is ready to be dispensed, the
beer is still working and giving off CO_2 gas and the
cask has to be spiled. A porous peg or spile is used to
close the cask and allow fermentation to proceed, and
at the correct time a hard peg is applied to close the
cask completely. The timing of this is one of the skills
of the landlord that are essential if the beer is to be in
perfect condition. The correct temperature is important, and in summer a cool cellar is an advantage. Find
a landlord who likes his draught bitter (and especially
if he has a good cellar) and you will be assured of a
good pint because he is more likely to have taken the
necessary amount of care.

Keg beers, on the other hand, have been processed
and matured at the brewery, and when delivered to
the pub are normally sterile. The containers can be
thrown around and the beer sold straight away. It is
because of their different characters that it is misleading and out of date to classify keg beers as draught
beers. The true draught beer has more character and
flavour and perhaps is the highest expression of the
brewer's art. A more practical and up-to-date defini-

tion of draught beer would be a 'beer which is sent out under finings, unfiltered and not artificially carbonated'.

This places the true draught beer (living) at one end of the scale and the keg beer (sterile) at the other, but there are still some beers that do not quite fit either definition and lie somewhere in between. Tank beers, for instance (p 19), often have the character of a draught beer although they are filtered—but nothing like so finely as a keg or bottled beer. So-called draught beers that are delivered from a depot but brewed in another part of the country may be adapted to some extent and the landlord can dispense them straight away on delivery, but they also lie somewhere in between a true living draught and a keg. Pre-fined beers (fined at the brewery and re-casked) and delivered bright may be hard to distinguish from a normal draught beer. Draught beers in take-home packs are often the normal draught beer adapted in some way—for instance by filtration—or they may be the bottled pale ale but with a reduced amount of CO_2.

A true draught and living beer can be bottled in a pub and taken home and drunk several weeks later and it is often better after the extra time for maturing. The bottle need not be completely filled to exclude air as the beer's own natural CO_2 will fill the space. In this way a draught beer has been known to keep perfectly for a year or more. A draught beer enthusiast can build up a cellar from all over the country on his travels and a beer-tasting evening at home will open the eyes of many people who think that it all tastes the same. This will, of course, no longer be possible if standardised national beers take over completely in years to come. It is a pity that people are being 'educated' to accept characterless imitations, because real draught bitter is one of the good things in life. Some comment about the beer being 'off' is often heard from someone (not used to a beer with character) encountering a true draught bitter for the first time. It is often forgotten that a beer with the name 'bitter' should also be bitter to the taste—if descriptive names mean anything at all.

Keg beer was pioneered in this country by Messrs Watney who first introduced it in 1933. It was originally conceived for outlets with intermittent trade like sports clubs where a draught beer which is not in continuous demand might lose quality through standing too long in contact with air. This problem was overcome by the development of sealed casks which were supplied with CO_2 gas to replace the air and which dispensed by the pressure of the gas on the beer (top pressure). The beer was not 'living' and fermentation and conditioning were completed prior to casking. As the cost of development was high and new equipment was needed, the brewers advertised these beers to sell to a much wider market and recover their costs. It is because of the high cost of advertising, the additional processes (chilling, filtering and pasteurising), as well as the new equipment, that they cost more than traditional draught beers. In brewer's language they may be described as premium (high-priced), high-quality (filtered and pasteurised and delivered bright) beers—terms which could be misinterpreted. Some keg beers do have some character, but they are usually regional beers designed for a local following. The pasteurisation process may have been omitted and the quantity and quality of the ingredients of course has a bearing on the end result. A distinctive palate, whilst pleasing some, may not appeal to others, so a beer aimed at a wide public on a national scale tends to lack character and so avoids giving offence to the majority of non-discriminating drinkers. These bland beers are sometimes described unlovingly as 'lemonade-type beers'.

To sum up the differences—keg beers are consistent, easy to handle, always bright, gassy, have a long shelf life after tapping, generally have little flavour or character and are more expensive than draught beers. Draught beers are usually well-flavoured with a distinctive character, normally consistent as uninterested landlords are not likely to keep their customers, vary in gassiness which is related to the dispensing system, have a limited shelf life after tapping (but untapped will keep better than non-living beers), cost less and are better value for money.

CONTAINER BEERS

These may be beers in sealed containers such as kegs or the name may be used to denote *tank beers*. These are draught beers which are conditioned in bulk and may be delivered in road tankers to large tanks in the pub or club. They are filtered—but not usually so finely filtered as keg or bottled beers—and may also be carbonated (artificially injected with CO_2 gas). They are approximately intermediate between true draught and keg beers and are convenient where the outlet does a very heavy trade and where delivery is over a long distance. They are probably sold as draught beers, and here again some customer orientation at the point of sale would not come amiss. They are 'bright beers', which is the term in use for beers that are completely clear. A draught beer becomes 'bright' after the finings have done their work.

BOTTLED BEER

These are treated in much the same way as keg beers but are normally more heavily carbonated and nearly always pasteurised. Naturally conditioned beers like Guinness, Worthington White Shield (and Bass Red Triangle still to be found) are now very few. These are the so-called sediment beers where a secondary fermentation has taken place in the bottle. They have not been filtered or pasteurised and in consequence are very-well-flavoured beers which require care in pouring (although the sediment is not harmful and some people prefer to tip it in, which makes the beer cloudy—but with a good yeasty flavour).

PALE ALE

This name embraces a whole family of beers described below, or it may refer more specifically to a bottled ale and some brewers call their draught bitter by this name. They are mostly pale in colour and well hopped although both these characters vary considerably.

Bitter: Usually a draught beer with a high hop rate which gives it the characteristic subtle bitter flavours which vary so much with the type of hops used. Often called 'ordinary', 'standard' or 'boy's bitter'. Some bitters now on the market are misnamed as they appeal more to a sweet tooth and in fact do not have a 'beery' palate at all. It is probably the bitter beers that give the most satisfaction to the beer-drinker and which exhibit the most marked variation in palate from different breweries.

Best bitter: Many brewers sell both an 'Ordinary' and

a 'Best'—names which are rather misleading. Best bitter (or 'Special') is stronger and therefore costs more and it may be sweeter (but not always). For bitterness (usually), lower cost and less alcohol the 'Ordinary' is 'best'—especially when a long, leisurely evening in the pub is contemplated. Some 'Ordinary' is as strong as other brewers' 'Best', and the name 'Ordinary' does not imply that it is beer of lower quality—although a 'high quality' beer often means, in brewer's language, a strongish beer. Which to drink depends on the effect desired from the drink, whether one's transport is horse-drawn or motorised, the depth of one's pocket and the sweetness of one's tooth. As there are instances of the 'Best' being more heavily hopped than the 'Ordinary', it is a good policy to try a half of each if the brew is unfamiliar.

Pale ale and light ale: These are usually bottled beers and both are really the same, but if there is both a pale and a light ale from the same brewer it can safely be assumed that the pale ale is the stronger of the two. Both these names can also be used to describe a draught bitter (e.g. Morrell's Light Ale and Brakspear's draught Pale Ale). Like bitters they vary quite considerably between different brewers. Old names for this type are *Family Ale* and *Dinner Ale*. *IPA India Pale Ale* is a name still used by some brewers, and it is a pale or bitter ale often above average strength. It was the name given by Bass in the early nineteenth century for the beer they exported to the East India Company. *AK* is a name sometimes given to a light bitter, or a light or dark mild. The origin of the name is obscure but one explanation is that at the beginning of the century beer duty was raised to an unprecedented level by Asquith's government. To counter this, special weak beers were brewed which were facetiously nicknamed 'Asquith's Knockout'. *Export* is the name often given to a strongish pale ale. *College Ale* is an old name for a strong beer brewed by monasteries and colleges of older universities. Some were known as *Audit Ales* which were brewed by the colleges especially for the day of audit. There used to be many other different ales connected with some rural festive occasion.

MILD ALE AND BROWN ALE

There are a number of light milds up and down the country which are more like light bitters. For instance, the Midlands are well known for their light milds. However, most milds are dark in colour, usually of lowish gravity and cost, and sweeter than pale ales (but there are also some quite dry dark milds and a true living draught mild will tend to become less sweet with time as fermentation proceeds in the cask). They are made from a proportion of darker malts, and caramel may be added. This is the dark product made by the action of heat (and sometimes ammonia) on sugar. They are less hopped than pale ales and often heavily primed—sugar added after fermentation and before casking. *Brown Ale* is the bottled form of mild ale which is sometimes known as 'home brewed'. Mild ales may be designated by a number of Xs, for instance 'XX Mild'. This is an old brewer's mark originally used by the monks, and the number of Xs relates to the quality. (But note that in the context of beer 'quality' may be related to strength, so a high-quality beer normally means a strong beer and does not mean that lesser-quality beers are inferior).

STRONG ALES

Most brewers produce a strong ale—a high gravity beer—of one kind or another, and they may be pale or dark in colour, sweet or dry. They may be draught or bottled beers and are matured over a longer period than a normal beer. Strong dark beers are *Burton Ales* (nothing to do with Burton-on-Trent), some *Scotch Ales* and *Old Ales*. As the name implies, old ales have been kept over a long period and have a characteristic bitterness—they are often brewed specially for the winter season. The well-known Newcastle Brown is a strong dark ale and not a brown ale. With these strong beers fermentation has been allowed to continue over a longer period (a month or more) and they may have a strength of 6-8 per cent of alcohol by volume. Again, their strength may be indicated by the number of Xs. *Stock Ales* are not so common now, and referred to strong ale matured over a long period. It was usually generously hopped and fermented out more or less to its limit, so that it would remain stable, and could be held in 'stock' almost indefinitely since it contained no residual nutrients to nourish spoilage organisms, and the plentiful hops and alcohol were there to provide a strong inhibitive effect. Its counterpart was a *Running Ale* which is again descriptive as it refers to beers which moved quickly—in other words, the average beer which used to be taken daily by most people. Today one could make comparisons with Strong and Best Bitters (although they are not Stock Ales but approaching them) and Ordinary Bitters representing Running Ales. (But note again that Ordinary Bitters are not inferior to Best Bitters). In *Diabetic* beers virtually no sugar is left because it has all been fermented away.

In the old days this was largely achieved by mashing at a lower temperature and then rolling the casks every day for months, gradually stuffing in more hops as for barley wines. Nowadays the same result can be achieved by using special strains of yeast or separate enzymes which have been extracted from moulds or bacteria—another case where scientific knowledge has speeded up the process and also brought it under more control. Diabetic or low-sugar beers may have an unusually high alcoholic content (eg Marston's Low-Cal; Whitbread Fremlins' Stock Ale).

The strongest beers of all are the *Barley Wines* which are matured, like wine, over a very long period—maybe up to eighteen months. They have a characteristic 'fruity' and very satisfying flavour and their strength may reach 10-11 per cent of alcohol by volume. Their palate varies considerably from brewer to brewer and they are extremely well balanced beers with a very long shelf life. The fermentation of barley wine is prolonged over a very long period by rolling the cask at frequent intervals keeping the yeast in suspension. Sometimes the cask is stuffed at intervals with hops which carry a certain amount of diastase (an enzyme which produces fermentable sugar) and yeasts. These help to 'nibble' at unfermented sugars, and the beer has usually reached stability when about 80 per cent of the dry solids originally in the wort have been fermented out—which is a very high figure. The hops contribute towards the delicate flavour of barley wines and are invaluable for their preservative property.

STOUT

This is dark, almost black, beer brewed from pale

malts but with a fair proportion of roasted barley or roasted malt. Stouts are well hopped in general, heavy in texture, and tend to have a sharp and bitter flavour. *Extra Stout*, as the name implies, is 'more so' and of a higher gravity. Sweet stouts are very common and used to be called *Milk Stout* because a non-fermentable sugar called lactose found in milk is used in its manufacture. The name is used no more because the administrators of the Trade Descriptions Act did not favour it. The story goes that Mackeson, the brewer in Hythe, Kent (which became wholly owned by the Whitbread group in the early sixties) who brewed a famous milk stout, allowed the farmer near the brewery a right of way for his cows. Visitors to the brewery were duly impressed when they saw the cows passing through the brewery yard. *Porter* was a popular drink in the eighteenth and nineteenth centuries and is still drunk in Ireland. It is half-way between a pale beer and a stout and is supposed to derive its name from its popularity with market porters in London.

LAGER

The name derives from the German word for store, and lager is stored to mature, sometimes for as long as a year. On the Continent of Europe lager is the most popular drink, and there are several important differences between the manufacture of lager and British-type beer. The fermentation takes place at a lower temperature—usually 41°-48°F or sometimes 50°-55°F, as opposed to 60°-68°F for ale. The yeast *Saccharomyces carlsbergensis* is used—a bottom-fermentation yeast which, after the initial formation of a small head, drops back through the wort. (British beer is manufactured by using *Saccharomyces cerev-isiae*, which is a top-fermentation yeast and rises to the top of the wort to form a thick head.) Then prolonged storage is usually given, seedless hops are used and the hopping rate is low. Different varieties of malt are used which give less full flavours than are obtained from ale malts. During the storage period the temperature is reduced to 32°F or less. This is the way lager is brewed by tradition, but perfectly good lager can be, and certainly is, brewed with top-fermenting yeast, other malts, or seeded hops—though perhaps not with all of these at once. A finer flavour is claimed for seedless hops, but it is doubtful whether a properly controlled direct comparison has been made between these and seeded hops. The prolonged period of storage can be shortened and the initial fermentation speeded up by a higher tempera-ture in the early stages, but the emphasis throughout, including consumption, is on lower temperatures. Lager is a refreshing drink with a not very strong but characteristic flavour. Throughout Europe lagers usu-ally—but not exclusively—are drunk, and it is all lager in the Americas and over most of the world including the Near and Far East. It is the same in Australia and New Zealand, although top-fermented beers are also brewed in those countries. In Britain lager is brewed by many brewers and is increasing in popularity, especially in hot weather. It is an ideal lunchtime drink as, being lighter and less hopped than beers, it is less sleep-inducing, but it does perhaps lack the full body and variety of flavours of top-fermented beers. That is by no means to say that all lagers taste alike, because there are a number of very distinctively flavoured lagers to be found.

The main types of lager are *Pilsner, Dortmund* and

Munich. Pilsner is pale in colour with a relatively high hop rate and is brewed with soft water. Dortmund is also pale but with less hops and harder water. Munich is a brown aromatic type with a fuller and sweeter palate. Different malts are used. The majority of imported lagers and most, if not all, lagers in Britain are of the Pilsner type.

Lager really comes from Munich, as it was there that a bottom-fermenting yeast was developed and then smuggled to Pilsen in Czechoslovakia by a Bavarian monk, and Pilsner was first brewed in 1842. Lager was brewed in Denmark in 1845 after the yeast had been acquired from Munich. In Britain a syndicate of six Manchester businessmen was formed to brew the 'beer' that was replacing top-fermented beer on the Continent, and for this purpose the Wrexham Lager Brewery was founded in 1882. It was later bought out by a gentleman called Robert Ferdinand Graesser. The Wrexham Lager Brewery sold several types of draught and bottled lagers and their pubs sold no other beers but stout. Several others soon brewed lager with little success until Barclays in 1921 and Graham's Golden Lager in the early thirties. Skol Lager is now brewed at Wrexham. Allsopps introduced lager to Burton around 1900 but after World War I transferred it to Alloa where Graham's Golden Lager was brewed.

3 DISPENSING SYSTEMS

The traditional image of the jovial landlord 'pulling a pint' with his hand round one of a set (usually three) of often gaily decorated hand bar pumps forming a centre-piece to his bar is in danger of becoming a dream of the past. These are the beer engine bar pumps, or 'pulls', and are a part of the beer engine which for many years has been the instrument by which the beer is pulled by suction from the cellar to the pint pot in the bar. They were designed so that one smooth pull delivered a half-pint of beer. Beer engine (or manual) bar pumps are decorative, very efficient and speedy. They are still quite widely used today, although many brewers are changing, or have changed, completely or partially to other systems. Many pubs used to, and some still do, dispense draught beer direct from the cask, and there are people (in the brewing industry) who consider this is the ideal system for true living draught beer provided the cask is kept in a cool place in the summer and is not too cold in the winter. If the cellar is a long way from the bar, beer engines are desirable. The drawback to both systems is that as the beer becomes lower in the cask its place is taken by air which eventually causes a degradation of the beer if trade is slack or the casks ordered were too big for the amount of likely trade. This is very rare and in most pubs with a normal turnover it is unlikely to happen because the air is never in contact with the beer for long enough to do any harm. Thorough cleanliness is vital with any system using pipes, as old yeast can quite easily lodge somewhere in the system and can spoil the beer. The danger of air spoiling the beer led brewers to look for other systems and now a bewildering variety of counter mountings can be seen on pub counters.

Beer is now very widely dispensed by so-called sophisticated systems of various kinds such as top pressure or electric pumps. In the top-pressure system the air is replaced by CO_2 (the natural gas given off by beer) which avoids the danger of the air spoiling the beer, but the CO_2 is also employed to push the beer up to the bar counter under pressure. Very often the pressure is too high, causing the beer to become very gassy, and what a frustrating business it is to a queue of thirsty drinkers when all that appears is a mass of froth and three or four glasses have to be brought into action by the landlord! Beer dispensed by top pressure nearly always has a different palate— what is often called a CO_2 bite. There are instances of landlords resisting 'progress' and retaining their old manual bar pumps or casks when other pubs owned by the same brewery have converted to top pressure. These landlords have experienced very satisfying increases in their trade, drinkers coming from afar to avoid a gassed-up pint. Seasoned beer-drinkers do not like the top pressure system, and the impression that a gassy beer (artificially carbonated) often has a different palate from the same beer containing only its own CO_2 does have some substance and a scientific explanation. CO_2 as a gas is odourless and tasteless, but when it dissolves in water it forms carbonic acid which has a slight sharpness and can over-stimulate the taste buds. In a beer with a small CO_2 content the volatile substances tend to evaporate off when CO_2 is blown through. These highly-flavoured compounds are in small quantities and easily volatile (i.e. become gas and are lost), so the beer is being fractionated. De-gassed beer which was previously over-gassed does not revert to its original condition flavourwise. The fact that CO_2 is the natural gas of beer does not seem to quite cover the situation. During the natural process of conditioning, CO_2 gas is given off, and if this is impeded or the reverse flow is enforced the conditioning process must be affected. A low gas pressure is safer and with a properly controlled system and the pressure not being too high the beer may be in perfect condition, but there seems to be a far greater risk of the beer being spoiled when dispensed by CO_2 pressure than with older systems. It would seem likely that with a deep cellar more pressure is required so there is more risk of the beer acquiring too much gas. In some systems the CO_2 gas is just for a light covering (to exclude air) and the beer is propelled by other means such as compressed air or electric pumps. These should avoid the risks, as there is no doubt that extraneous CO_2 forced into the beer nearly always masks or eliminates its characteristic and delicate flavours. Some licensees dislike handling the gas cylinders, which they normally have to purchase themselves, and they have been known to explode if not correctly used.

Electric pumps are widely used, especially in the midlands and north of England. There is usually a counter mounting that dispenses exactly half a pint, and is in the form of a glass cylinder or sphere which becomes refilled after each half pint is dispensed. The only drawback to an electric system seems to be that thirsty would-be drinkers are likely to remain thirsty should there be a power cut. Using electricity, compressed air may be used as the motive power, but it does not come into contact with the beer which has a light covering of CO_2. Special taps are available which can influence the amount of head on the beer to suit local preferences. There are instances of the old manual bar pumps being retained and used in conjunction with electric pumps which provide the motive power for most of the time. When the power goes off the beer engine is connected and nobody goes thirsty. The pump handles add to the decorative appeal of the bar.

Electric systems can usually be recognised by the glass container on the bar which is filled with beer. There are cases where the tap is directly below a beer engine pump on the bar which is not itself used and the beer is dispensed by top pressure—a fact which could be missed. It is also known for the beer to be passed in a pipe, through a wooden cask, giving the impression that it is 'beer from the wood'. Top pressure beer can usually be distinguished by excessive froth, a head with tiny bubbles and a sharp taste. If the would-be drinker in a strange pub favours one system or another a good policy would be to ask the landlord when ordering.

4   BEER FROM THE WOOD

There are many people who think that beer from the wood has a special flavour that no other container can give. A wooden cask certainly has an attractive Olde Worlde look, and perhaps the impression of a special flavour is influenced by its nostalgic appeal. What are the true facts, and why are wooden casks largely being replaced by casks made from metal?

There are a number of reasons for this change, perhaps the most important being that wooden casks cannot be completely sterilised. There are so many tiny nooks and crevices in which the 'spoiling bugs' can hide and can manage to survive all normal cleaning operations. The art of manufacture of wooden casks (cooperage) is centuries old, very skilful and requires an apprenticeship of several years. Although skilled coopers are still to be found—some are employed by brewers who still supply beer from the wood, and there may be many now out of work or otherwise employed—in the future there may well be a shortage. Wooden casks must be made individually, for which special tools are required; they cannot be mass-produced. Metal casks are tougher, last longer and are also lighter. Added to all this is the fact that the special type of oak wood required comes from abroad and is said to be getting more scarce.

On the other hand, wooden casks do have the advantage that if they are left in the hot sun it will be several hours before the warmth affects the beer inside, because it is so well insulated. Then it is known that a wooden cask develops its own microflora ('bugs' of many kinds which are not always of the 'spoiling' variety) including various yeasts and these certainly have some effect on the flavour of the beer with which they come in contact. Most seasoned beer drinkers have experienced that superb flavour that occasionally comes from a 'good' barrel and have wondered whether it was imagination or perhaps just the contrast between beer from that barrel and some particularly tasteless beer they may have just drunk. Sometimes the effect is bad and the barrel has to be discarded, but this does not happen very often to brewers who still retain the use of wooden casks. These brewers, it may be noted, brew well hopped beers and hops have a marked preservative value, so a well hopped beer provides its own protection. Quite a number of modern beers tend to lack the rich, fruity, beery flavours of those of yesteryear and would be particularly prone to attack by the various organisms lying in wait in a wooden cask. Many brewers themselves prefer beer from wooden casks and it is considered by many experts that they confer a longer life on a true draught beer because it is able to breathe.

Page 33 (*above*) Brewery and maltings (Belhaven, near Dunbar, Scotland); (*below*) inside a traditional maltings. The barley grains are being turned and spread on the floor to control the temperature of the growing malt

Page 34 (*above*) **Adding** hops to the wort in the copper; (*below*) wort being boiled with the hops in the copper

Wooden casks are still in use for spirits and wines. Most of the better table wines are stored in oak casks for about two years during which time the wine can pick up certain characteristics, such as extra tannin and vanillin, from the oak. No other container has been found that allows the wine to come into contact with very slight amounts of oxygen that make a wine mature properly. Metal casks are now replacing some of the oak casks in the wine industry, but it is doubtful whether this will be so for the better-quality wines. This all supports the argument, of course, that wooden barrels do give beer a little bit of what's needed—perhaps rather a little extra 'something', because superb beer is also stored and dispensed from metal casks. Some wooden casks have an inner metal lining—easier to clean, but the beer from these is not true 'beer from the wood'.

As is often the case, there are two seemingly valid viewpoints, and one thing is sure—wooden casks with their nostalgic appeal will remain with us as long as there are coopers still plying their ancient trade and brewers still willing to go to a little extra trouble.

5   COOL BEER—IS IT BEST?

There has never been any shortage of complaints from visitors from overseas about Britain's lukewarm beers. This is easy to understand because the selfsame visitors have come from countries where lager is the normal tipple and lager should be served at cool temperatures. A warm lager is a repellant drink, but so is a top-fermented beer when it is drunk at too low a temperature, as it loses most of its character. All American beer is lager, but you do not ask for a

lager in the USA: you ask for a beer—and get a lager.
An American visiting Britain who asks for a beer will
receive a beer and will probably be unimpressed at its
comparatively warm temperature.

The fact is that the temperature at which beer
should be drunk to achieve the fullest possible benefit
is related to the fermenting temperature. The best
temperature at which to drink lager is 45°-50°F
(7°-10°C) at which temperature range it will be at its
best with the flavour achieving its fullest expression.
In some parts of the world lager is served so cold that
it hurts the eyeballs. and although it may be very
refreshing otherwise, the character of that particular
choice brew is almost completely lost. To obtain the
best from top-fermented beers they should be served
at a range of 50°-60°F (10°-15°C). 55°F (13°C) is
reckoned to be ideal.

6 BRIGHT BEER—IS IT BEST?

Visual drinking is the order of the day, and brewers'
advertisements emphasise clarity and sparkle. The
beers that look so good may not taste so good
because they might be filtered and some of the
goodness and source of flavour removed. Many a
good pint has been returned and thrown away
because it has a slight haze and was not as clear as it
was considered it should be. A protein haze can
develop if beer is chilled, but the chances are that a
cloudy pint of draught beer is caused by a small
quantity of yeast which has not settled. In neither
case would any harm result (people pay good money
for yeast tablets) and some of the best pints that have
been consumed by man have been cloudy—provided
it is not beer that is not really ready and conditioned.

Good advice would be to try a sip with the eyes shut before returning it to the landlord.

7 THE FLAVOUR OF BEER

The fact that there is a wide difference in the flavour of beers has often been discounted and it is true that differences between lagers are often very fine and may only be detectable by a sensitive palate. But certain lagers are quite easily distinguishable, for instance Scandinavian lagers seem to possess a certain style and are different from German lagers. Swiss lagers have their own particular character. Jamaican lager is distinctive, so is lager from Thailand, and some lagers are dark in colour. English lager is different in general from, for instance, lager from South Australia, and one could continue with many more examples. Nevertheless differences are more acute and vary on a much smaller geographical scale with top-fermented beers. As an instance, Dorset is not a very large county yet it has four brewers all producing draught bitters with their own character and which are quite easily distinguishable.

In fact there is a remarkable variety of draught and bottled beers up and down the country yet it is extraordinary how conservative many beer-drinkers are and how intolerant to unaccustomed brews. Perhaps the consumer is being conditioned to goods (not only beer) with little or no flavour, so that a well-flavoured article has become, in many cases, unacceptable. One rarely hears of gourmets who do not like a variety of, for instance, cheeses; nor do wine connoisseurs limit their tippling to a favourite château or vineyard. It is of course sometimes difficult to seek out other brews when living in an area largely monopolised by one brewer, and unfortunately many free houses seem to use little imagination or enterprise when choosing their 'beer cellar'. However it is well worth developing a liberal attitude towards beer because with the information given in this book many different kinds can be found, and even many bottled beers have interesting characters and are worth collecting when away, for later drinking at home.

It would be very surprising if all beers did taste alike, when all the different variables are considered—brewing techniques, hops and blends of hops, yeasts, malts and brewing environments. In fact national brewers have to go to great pains to ensure that their national beers which are served throughout the country are identical although brewed at several centres. This is quite possible by achieving 100 per cent sterilisation of the brewing equipment, by having it entirely enclosed from the outside, completely avoiding the influence of the environment such as local wild yeasts. Identical ingredients and brewing techniques must of course be employed.

At the other end of the scale, a true draught beer can vary slightly from pub to pub and from brewery to brewery and is more subject to slight environmental differences. A deep, cool cellar is ideal for keeping the beer well-insulated from changes in the outside temperature. There are sometimes subtle variations in the draught beer in the same pub, and, discounting unclean pipes which can ruin beer but are not very common, there is the occasional cask which may seem to be outstanding. As explained on p 32 this may be caused by the cask's own microflora.

If the ultra-modern drinker of tomorrow finds

himself with one national beer, no doubt sweet and quite characterless, he will have two consolations. There will no longer be the 'difficult' problem of what to drink, and he can always resort to home-brewing from time to time to remind himself of what beer should really taste like.

8 GRAVITY AND STRENGTH

All too often people find themselves confused when referring to original gravity (OG) and alcoholic strength. It should be understood that gravity is only one of several factors affecting the alcoholic strength of beer, all of which are inter-related. Original gravity refers to the gravity of the wort at the beginning of the brewing process and it is concerned only with identifying how much solid material has been dissolved. This solid material consists mainly of the natural sugars from the malted barley which have been infused or 'mashed' in hot liquor. This material is the food upon which the yeast thrives during the fermentation process.

Fermentation is always stopped when a certain level of sugar remains in the beer, and how much remains depends upon the balance in the finished product that the brewer wishes to achieve. Thus, within practical limits, it is possible to produce a heavy gravity beer with a low alcoholic strength and a light gravity beer with a high alcoholic strength. But the latter would have a much drier flavour balance than the former.

So far as alcoholic strength is concerned, this is normally expressed as a percentage of the beer, which is simply what it is. A 3 per cent beer would be one which contained 3 per cent of alcohol measured either by weight or by volume.

In Britain the strength of beer is usually measured by its original gravity (OG) and this is the specific gravity prior to fermentation. Specific gravity is the weight of a solution compared with the weight of an equal volume of water at the same temperature, and water for brewing purposes is rated as 1000. It is measured by an instrument called a saccharometer. Wort or beer gravity is expressed, for convenience, as the specific gravity with the decimal point left out. For example a beer with an SG (or OG if prior to fermentation) of 1·037 would be expressed as 1037 degrees or often just 37 degrees.

The average gravity of the nation's beers is published annually in the Report of HM Customs & Excise, and for the past ten years the average has been around 1037, approximately three degrees higher than twenty years ago.

As already pointed out, there is only a partial relationship between gravity and alcoholic strength and the two cannot be related under any specific rule. However, as a rough guide and provided the beer is of normal composition and has been attenuated—i.e. fermented out—to normal limits, then one can take the excess OG, shift the decimal one place to the right and end up with something close to the percentage of alcohol by volume. For example 1037 degrees OG would give about 3·7 per cent alcohol by volume.

Because the original gravity is only one of the factors relating to the alcoholic strength of the beer and furthermore does not reflect the quality of the raw materials used in its preparation, nearly all brewers have considered that it would be misleading to declare the original gravity on bottle labels.

On the other hand it would be quite a useful guide to the public if more brewers did publish the OG on the label or beer dispenser (only Northern Clubs' Federation Brewery does this at present, although some brewers are quite open about it) because it does give an indication of potential strength, and one can quite easily become 'one over' through drinking the normal quantity of an unfamiliar beer. It will be realised that the eventual specific gravity (ie after fermentation) will be less than the OG, and with strong ales and barley wines the degree of attenuation can vary tremendously with the type of yeast used, the mashing temperature and the composition of the grist and other things.

Some typical figures (from the laboratory of an analytical chemist) are given below (figures are expressed in degrees).

	Barley wine		Strong ale	
	SG	OG	SG	OG
Example A.	1014·2	1078·9	A. 1016·7	1080·9
B.	1033·3	1102·6	B. 1014·7	1078·6
C.	1013·9	1073·6	C. 1016·3	1067·3

The point is illustrated by strong ale B which ended up with a lower gravity than C although its OG was higher. This pinpoints the difficulty of declaring the OG, and although the gravity of the final product may vary very slightly between brews, these do not seem sufficient reasons for giving no indication of the strength of a beer—either before or after fermentation.

When comparing the strength of beer with wines and spirits it is necessary to understand the term 'proof spirit'. This is a frequent source of confusion. Before the nineteenth century, a mixture of alcohol and water was called proof spirit if it would just burn or allow gunpowder to explode after wetting. This was taken as standard and the test was supposed to be 'proof' that the mixture contained a minimum percentage of alcohol. Fortunately it has not been necessary for distillers to risk blowing themselves and their distilleries into kingdom-come when testing their latest distillation because a twentieth-century Act thoughtfully expressed the phrase in more up-to-date terms. This Act says 'Spirits shall be deemed to be proof if the volume of the ethyl alcohol contained therein made up to the volume of the spirits with distilled water has a weight equal to that of twelve-thirteenths of a volume of distilled water equal to the volume of the spirits, the volume of each liquid being computed as at 51 degrees Fahrenheit'. A very profound declaration which in slightly less perplexing terms means that proof spirit is defined as 57·06 per cent by volume or 49·24 per cent by weight of ethyl alcohol in water at 51 degrees Fahrenheit. Stronger or weaker spirits are 'under' or 'over' proof.

This means that 2 per cent proof spirit, above which excise must be paid on beers, is 1·14 per cent alcohol, by volume (57·06 multiplied by 2 and divided by 100).

Applying these figures to a typical draught bitter with an alcoholic strength (by volume) of 4 per cent, this becomes 6·99 per cent proof or 7 in round figures. An average whisky of 70 per cent of proof spirit is therefore about ten times as strong as an average draught beer, taking equal volumes. Most British beers contain between 2·5 per cent and 5 per cent of alcohol by volume but strong ales and barley wines may be as much as 10 per cent or more, which is in the table wine league.

Proof spirit is based on a simpler system in the

USA and means a mixture of equal volumes of alcohol and water, so that an American whisky of 80 per cent proof has 40 per cent of alcohol by volume.

Typical figures for a range of beers are given below, the figures expressed in percentage of alcohol by volume:

Draught bitter 3·0-4·5
Draught mild 2·5-3·5
Light ale   3·0-4·0
Pale ale 4·0-6·5
Brown ale 2·5-3·5
Stout   3·5-5·0
Strong ales and barley wines 6·0-10·0
Lager   3·0-4·0
Strong lager   6·0-8·0

CHAPTER 2

The Brewer's Art

During the Middle Ages beer was the staple drink, partly, perhaps, because the water supply was often not safe to drink. From that period to the present the art of malting and brewing has developed into a science, brewers now are often qualified chemists, and thousands of pages have been written on the subject.

With the popularity of home brewing and the increasing number of home-brew kits (with very simple instructions) on the market, some people think that brewing is not so difficult after all. So what is the difference between the home brewer and the commercial brewer? In order to produce a consistent brew—and no 'bad' beer leaves a brewery (or very rarely): it is usually what happens afterwards that causes something to go wrong—the basic ingredients must be the same. The brewer selects his hops and blend of hops and his malted barley with infinite care. He does not take just anything that happens to be available, and it is the same with his sugars. The home brewer cannot usually do this. He takes what is in the kit, and the ingredients may always come from the same source, but he is not in such control of the situation. If the home brewer buys his hops separately he cannot easily ensure that they are always exactly the same. Malt extracts, which are the most common form of malt for home brews, are not made with flavour in mind. The commercial brewer can adjust the composition of the wort in the mash tun by changing the temperature of the wort, but when using an extract the mash tun stage has passed. Home brewing is often done under rather variable conditions and not rigidly controlled (this does not, of course, apply to all home brewers). The commercial brewer controls the temperature in the mash tun to within 1°F and often to within half a degree, and he can decide exactly at what point to stop the fermentation from proceeding further. The home brewer usually ferments right out, though leaving some of the wort unfermented or having a proportion of unfermentable sugars gives body to the beer. If a large number of different grades of extract were available there would be more scope for the home brewer; however, most home brews are eminently drinkable and better and more tasty than a number of commercial beers. The commercial brewer cannot always brew what he would like to brew, as economic considerations and the demands of the market created by advertising often dictate his brewing activities. The result may not always be what he himself would have liked.

Beer is made only from malt, hops, sugar, yeast and water. It may be that a chemical or chemicals have been used in certain instances to create a good head on the beer, but no one has yet succeeded (thank goodness) in synthesising it artificially. Researchers have tried to find a means of making a beer concentrate, perhaps a powdered beer, so far without success—but the day may yet come, and no doubt under the banner of progress. Many beers have of course been sweetened, cereals other than barley have been used and hop extracts have been used instead of the natural hop, but probably most beers are still made from the same natural ingredients as have been used for centuries.

Malt is the basic ingredient for the manufacture of beer, and for hundreds of years the maltster has made the best malt from the best barley. There are several reasons why barley is the most suitable cereal. Firstly it has always been considered that malted barley produces the most desirable flavours. Barley has a husk which maize and wheat do not have, and this husk forms a filter bed when the malt is mashed in the brewery, which is an essential part of the brewing process. Also barley is the most readily available cereal in the UK. With wheat malt the germ breaks easily, allowing undesirable moulds to flourish. But for one reason or another cereals other than barley are in use and certainly have some influence—not always bad—on the palate of the beer. Some wheat beers in Germany are labelled as such and have quite a different palate from barley beers. There may be a case for the declaration of ingredients by brewers.

The malting process itself is a very skilful operation and consists of a controlled germination of the barley which is finally stopped by heat. The hard barley is transformed into tender malt with a pleasant biscuity flavour, but the malted grain has the same outward appearance as the original barley. The insoluble starch in the barley corn is converted during germination into soluble starch which the brewer can easily convert into a fermentable sugar solution. Finally the malt is 'screened' to remove the rootlets which form during germination. Traditional maltings are very conspicuous buildings, and it is in these that the maltster soaked the barley in water for about sixty hours and then spread the grains on the malting floor in a thick and even layer to await germination. The art of the maltster was to control the temperature of the growing malt with the greatest care by turning and spreading the barley with various shovels and forks. The maltster often walked barefoot on the malting floors to avoid damage to the growing grains which could then become mouldy. The process of flooring lasted about ten days after which the temperature was allowed to rise to about 68°F (20°C) to stop further growth. The 'green' malt was then loaded on to a kiln where it was dried. The purpose of this was to stop the growth and to cure the malt which gave it its characteristic biscuity flavour. This was a very critical operation before thermometers came to the aid of the maltster, because the temperature had to be high enough to cure the malt but not too high, otherwise the enzymes in the embryo would be destroyed (they would be necessary in the brewing process to come, for converting the starch into sugar). This is the basic malting process and it is the same today except that modern methods have become very scientific and mechanised. The modern maltster may treat his barley with certain additives which give him more control over the germination, and temperatures as high as 210°F may be needed for roasted malt. Many brewers still use malt made by traditional methods without short cuts, but the old art is gradually disappearing.

The hop plant is treated in more detail in another

chapter (p 54), but it is worth mentioning here that hop extracts are being used to some extent in brewing at the present time. The purpose of adding hops to beer is, firstly, to add to the beer's flavour—the pleasant 'hoppy', bitter palate which varies so much with different varieties and blends of varieties. This flavour comes from the oils and resins which are in the hop flower, or cone as it is called. Then, hops have a very important preservative function because certain hop constituents have antiseptic properties and they assist in the formation of the head on beer. The spent hops act as a filter bed in the hop-back and remove some of the protein which has been precipitated by the tannin in the hops during boiling. This protein would give the beer a hazy appearance. Hop extracts are sometimes used because they are more economical—they are less bulky, for one thing. The chemistry of the flavour and preservative value of hops is extremely complicated and is not yet completely understood. Hop extracts contain the important alpha acids which give bittering power. They probably do not contain all the valuable oils, resins and tannins present in a hop cone and cannot give the aroma and flavour that the natural hop produces. Beer made with hop extract is like meat without salt. It is of course possible that research will eventually enable a greater understanding to be gained of the flavour given by the hop cone, and hop extracts will most likely continue to improve. But it is doubtful whether a beer made solely with extract and no natural hops at all would achieve the quality of a beer made in the traditional manner.

The next ingredient to be used in the brewing of beer is sugar, which was first used as a cheap source of fermentable material. It is possible to brew without sugar added at all and in Germany there is a Pure Beer Act which prohibits its use. Sugar contributes towards the body of the beer, but with lager, which is fairly thin anyway, it does not matter so much. There are a whole variety of sugars available to the brewer which give him great scope. As they are free from protein, their use dilutes the wort with respect to haze-forming materials. Sugar in various forms can be added at different stages of the brewing process to give flavour, colouring (caramel) and of course additional fermentable matter. The chemistry of sugar is very complicated and there are many varieties and chains of sugars with varying degrees of fermentability. A high proportion of unfermented sugar left in the wort after fermentation would contribute towards the body of the beer. Priming sugars may be added to draught beers before they leave the brewery to encourage a secondary fermentation. Wort with a high proportion of malt sugar has a balanced spectrum of fermentable and unfermentable material (giving body) and additional sugar may be for economic reasons and to adjust the original gravity.

Yeast is not, strictly speaking, an ingredient of beer, rather is it a catalyst or agent. It is the fermenting agent which feeds on the sugars, converting most of them into carbon dioxide and alcohol. During fermentation the yeast cells are very busy and they reproduce themselves many times resulting in the great thick creamy head at the top of the fermenting vessel. They generate a considerable amount of heat which has to be carefully controlled otherwise the beer's flavour will be spoilt, and this is one reason for failures in home brews—the fermentation is too fast. Surplus yeast is sold off for the manufacture of yeast extracts and yeast tablets. There are many different strains including wild yeasts, and no brewer wants his brewery to be the haven of any wild yeast at all if he can help it. Some of them are quite capable of ruining his beer. Yeasts are examined by the brewer under his microscope and some unwanted strains look very like the home team. However, they do not act the same, and when a contaminating strain enters the brewery a tremendous cleaning and sterilising operation in the brewery has to be undertaken. Sometimes a yeast strain may 'go off' and then the brewer has to start again with a fresh yeast from another brewery. It has even been known for a wild yeast in residence in the brewery to be responsible for the pleasant character and flavour of the beer from that brewery, in which case it is a welcome guest. It is obvious from all this that yeast has another very important function—it has a considerable influence upon flavour.

Water in a brewery is known as liquor, and in the past—and still today—many breweries had their own water supply from a well or wells in the brewery itself, but nowadays the town supply is mostly used. In bygone years certain areas became noted for their beers and it was all to do with the water supply. Perhaps the best-known is the brewing town of Burton-on-Trent which was famous for its production of pale ales, and the local water containing calcium sulphate (or gypsum) in good proportions was just what was needed for these beers. London became noted for its stouts because the water contained a sufficiency of calcium carbonate and sodium chloride (salt). Nowadays water can be easily adjusted by the addition or subtraction of salts to suit the brewer's requirements.

It would seem that the ingredients of beer have an influence upon the severity of hang-over suffered. Some beers appear to be more lethal in their after-effects than others. Research has been rather limited in this direction, but it is known that alcohols and esters (fusil alcohols) formed during fermentation—other than ethyl alcohol—are largely responsible for the 'morning-after' feeling. The type of malt and yeast and also the hops and hop rate can all have some bearing, but knowledge at present is rather imprecise. Many people have found that the more gassy beers give the worst after-effects.

Brewing itself has changed little basically over the years. It is now more scientifically controlled and large computerised breweries or beer factories have been erected with space-age control panels. Continuous fermentation techniques have been evolved. Traditional breweries were on the tower pattern and use was made of gravity in moving the liquor on some of its journeys.

Brewing can be conveniently summarised into six main operations, which are milling, mashing, boiling, cooling, fermenting and racking. In the first operation the malt is lightly crushed in a mill to crack the husk so that water can reach the starch inside during the next stage of mashing. The ground malt has now become grist, in brewing parlance. It is then mixed with hot liquor, which is called mashing, and the resulting mash is run into the mash tun. This is a large vessel and has a slotted or false bottom so that the liquor can run through it, but at this stage it is something like porridge so it stays put for about two hours, giving time for the enzymes in the malt to convert the starch to malt sugar. During this time temperature control is very critical and a variation of

as little as 1°F can affect the quality of the
end-product. An enzyme, incidentally, is a naturally
produced catalyst or chemical agent, and different
kinds are present in most living organisms. At the end
of mashing the taps are opened and hot liquor is
sprayed or 'sparged' over the mash for 3-4 hours and
the resulting extract passes through to the coppers
where hops and perhaps sugars are added. In the
meantime the mash has changed its name and become
the wort (pronounced 'wert'). The spent grain in the
mash tun has had all the sugars washed out of it and
is sold as an animal feeding-stuff often known as
brewer's grains.

Now the wort is in the copper, where it is boiled
for some 1-2 hours together with the hops and sugar
carefully selected by the brewer for the particular
flavour he wants. There are several reasons for boiling
the wort. Firstly the oils and resins are thereby
extracted from the hops. Then the wort is sterilised
and all enzyme activity is halted. It is also a means of
controlling the strength of the finished beer, because
the longer it is boiled the more evaporation there will
be and the more concentrated and stronger will be
the resultant wort. The two-hour boil is also
important for the retention of unfermentable solids
in the beer to give a good body and avoid a runaway
fermentation.

The mixture of wort and hops is now pumped
through another vessel with a perforated false bottom
called a hop-back which strains off the wort from the
spent hops, which are sold as hop manure. The wort
is now almost ready for fermentation but it must first
be cooled to about 60°F, as yeast would not survive
at much above 70°F. So it is passed through heat
exchangers which cool it, then on into the fermenting

vessel. The yeast is now added and the day's brewing is finished; it has probably taken 10-12 hours. It is at this stage, before fermentation commences, that the man from the ministry, in this case the Customs and Excise Officer, judges the quantity and specific gravity (the OG or original gravity) on which the duty to be paid is based.

Fermentation takes about a week, during which time surplus yeast is skimmed off and the remainder left to form a natural barrier against airborne infection. The beer is then racked into casks (eg for draught beer) where further slow fermentation proceeds in the presence of residual yeast, carbon dioxide (CO_2) gas is given off, and the beer becomes conditioned. At the same time undesirable flavours disappear and desirable flavours are developed. Instead of casks the beer may be racked into conditioning tanks (for bottling and kegging), where, after a time, it is chilled and filtered and may also be pasteurised.

CHAPTER 3

The Hop Plant

Hop is the name given to a number of species of plant belonging to the genus *Humulus*. They are twining, perennial plants in the same family as the stinging nettle (family Urticaceae, 'if it stings you, it 'urts you!'—not that hops do sting).

The hops used in beer are the mature cones (or flowers) of the common hop, *Humulus lupulus*, and its many varieties. It has been used almost exclusively for brewing for 1,200 years or more, and there is evidence that it has been used in Eastern Europe as a yeast preservative in baking and in brewing for 2,000 years or more. Hopped beer first reached England from the Low Countries in the early part of the fifteenth century, and boiling hops with the wort had become the general practice by the sixteenth century. The value of the hop cones in brewing stems from the essential resins, oils and tannins present in the glands called *lupulin* at the base of the bracts of the cone. The resins are responsible for the bitterness and preservative qualities; the hop oils confer a delicate flavour and aroma; and the tannins assist in the precipitation of protein which could otherwise cause a slight haze in the beer. In fact the chemistry of the flavour and preservative value of the hops is extremely complicated and there is still much scope for further investigation. As has been mentioned before, hop extracts are commonly used nowadays. They are convenient and economical, but are by no means a proper substitute for the natural hop. Present-day extracts may confer a bittering flavour, but they do not give the full aroma and flavour of the natural hop.

The common hop is a climbing perennial plant which may produce for as long as 10-20 years. It has a large rootstock, and this 'hill' or 'stock' has many vegetative buds which give rise to shoots (often called bines). New bines are produced each season, and die after maturity. New hop fields (called hop gardens in south-east England and hop yards in the West Midlands) are created from root cuttings or sections of underground stems, and the young vines or bines are trained to climb strings which are renewed annually and are supported by a permanent framework of wooden poles and wires. They have a phenomenal speed of growth and under favourable conditions can grow six inches or more in twenty-four hours, but the growth-rate is very much dependent on the weather.

The hop is called dioecious, which means that the male and female flowers are on separate plants. The male flower is very small and burr-like and appears in July, and the cone is the fruit which develops on the female plant after flowering. It is 2-4 inches long with overlapping yellowish-green bracts or scales. Cones may be produced without seeds by the exclusion of male plants from the hop gardens, or with seeds by planting male plants at a rate of one to 100 or 200 female plants. Seeded hops are grown in England and seedless hops on the Continent. An advantage of seedless hops is that the brewer does not have to pay for the weight of the seeds, which may be as high as 15 per cent. By tradition they have always been used for the brewing of lager, so most countries prefer them to seeded hops. However, they are not essential for lager-brewing, and although most hops for lager are imported, English brewers do also use seeded hops for some of their lager. It has been claimed that seedless hops give a finer flavour, but no direct comparison has been made and the claim is unsubstantiated. Seeded hops could be a nuisance in continental brewing techniques, but there would seem to be no advantage in changing to seedless hops in Britain as there is already a tremendous difference in flavour between varieties. Actually it would be virtually impossible, because as anyone who has examined a Kentish hedgerow would realise, wild male hops are growing all over the hop-growing countryside.

The hop cones ripen during August and September and nearly all the picking is now done by machines. At this time they contain 65-80 per cent of moisture and they have to be dried down to a moisture content of 10 per cent. If they were not dried they would be certain to heat up, discolour and go off. In England the hops are dried in brick buildings with a tapering roof surmounted by a pivoted wooden cowl which helps to prevent a back draught in windy weather. These buildings are called oast-houses. After drying, the hops are stored for several days for curing, when the moisture content is equalised throughout the cone, which becomes tougher and more pliable for baling or bagging.

Brewers who do not own hop gardens have to buy their annual requirement from a hop merchant who may have a large number of small packets from each farm, and the selection of the exact quality depends upon the skill of the brewer. On the Continent the merchant buys up the entire crop of a larger number of growers who partially dry their harvest, and then the merchant finishes off the drying and packs them himself. In this way the Continental merchant has large quantities of the same quality.

Hops like rich, alluvial and well-drained soils and are grown commercially in Australia, Belgium, Czechoslovakia, England, France, Japan, New Zealand, South Africa, South America, Spain, Poland, the USA, the USSR and Yugoslavia. The USA is the biggest producer and this country together with Germany and England account for about three-quarters of the world total, which is in the region of 150,000 acres. In England about 20,000 acres are grown, most of which are in Kent, then the West Midlands (Herefordshire and Worcestershire), then North Hampshire. Hops are not grown north of the Midlands because they like a warmish climate; neither do they grow in the tropics.

The hop cone has a delightful fresh smell which is very familiar to residents of brewing towns. Not everyone may find it agreeable but it would be hard to dispute that a hop garden in summer with its attendant oast-houses is a part of the rural scene that adds piquancy to the hop-growing countryside.

CHAPTER 4

The Brewer's Dray

The most familiar symbol of the brewing industry in the past was, perhaps, the giant dray-horse pulling its load of beer barrels and making an impressive sight in the brewing towns of bygone years. Today they can still be seen at agricultural shows and even delivering beer in several towns up and down the country. And what a colourful sight they are! Some brewers have reasoned that, apart from any prestige value, they have other advantages for local deliveries within a few miles of the brewery. When a horse is held up at traffic lights he is resting, but a lorry is burning up expensive fuel; and if a dray-horse could speak he would surely support such a logical argument, because they seem to enjoy their work which they perform with pride and a touch of dignity.

The brewer's dray-horse belongs to one of the five main types of modern horses—the Draught (or 'Heavy' or 'Work' or 'Cart') horse. (The other types are Saddle, Light Harness, Heavy Harness and Ponies, and each of these types includes various breeds.) Draught horses are large, bulky and tall. They are strong and were bred for industry, and for pulling ploughs and waggons.

Perhaps the most famous of the heavy breeds is the Shire, which hails from central and north-east England and is a descendent of the war-horses of the Middle Ages. The Shire is usually bay or brown—less often black or grey—with great tufts of hair or 'feather' on the pastern (the section of the foot between fetlock and hoof). It was commonly used both as a farm and dray-horse and can still be seen today delivering Thwaites' beers in the Lancashire town of Blackburn, and in London taking casks of Young & Co's beers to thirsty customers around Wandsworth and Whitbread's beers to parched denizens of the East End. In the south-west a shire type delivers out of Plymouth Breweries, which now belongs to Courage Ltd; and in Leeds, Tetley uses them on town deliveries.

Another breed used for pulling brewer's waggons is the Percheron, which hailed from La Perche in Normandy and is a composite of the medieval Great Horse and French Coach Horse with some oriental ancestry. It has shortish legs without hair and its colour is grey or black. Percherons deliver the beer of Vaux & Associated Breweries in Sunderland and Edinburgh (Thos. Usher) and also Adnams' Ales in and around Southwold in Suffolk.

The Suffolk or Suffolk Punch is another typical heavy English breed originating in Suffolk and existing as far back as the sixteenth century. Its colour is a uniform light or dark chestnut with a flaxen mane and tail and it is the only clean-legged British draught horse. Although Suffolks were more often used on the farm than for delivering the stuff required to quench the thirst of our ancestors, it was not so long ago that they could be seen delivering

Truman's beers in London's East End. Now they have been relegated to the comparative peace of the Essex countryside around Colchester.

The Clydesdale is a native of Lanarkshire, but is said to have been founded by a Dutch stallion brought from England in the eighteenth century. It is usually brown or black with prominent white markings and long fetlocks with feather. It is the breed which the Hull Brewery has used for many years—and still uses—for local deliveries in the town.

These are not the only breeds, and countries such as Belgium, France, Holland and Russia developed their own styles of work-horses with individual characteristics which, unfortunately, are becoming less and less common. They may be an enigma to some motorists in a hurry, but when he hears those impatient hoots on the horn the old dray-horse will not take much notice—he can't go any faster. Perhaps the pressure of modern traffic will, in the end, relegate the few remaining teams to the showground. That will be a pity and the loss of a colourful symbol of the past.

CHAPTER 5

The Brewing Industry - changes and trends

In the early 1880s there were nearly 17,000 'brewers for sale' (wholesale brewers) and over 70,000 other brewers (which included home-brewed houses, such people as farmers brewing for themselves and their employees, college brewers, etc). By the early part of the twentieth century the figures were down to some 6,000 brewers for sale and about twice that number of other brewers. The numbers have since taken a headlong dive. The 1961-2 *Brewery Manual* listed just over 180 independent brewers (that is, brewers who are not under the control of another brewing company). Takeover activities continued in the sixties and by 1967 less than 120 independently operating brewers were listed. The numbers of 'other brewers' fell at an even faster rate until by mid-1972 the brewing industry in Britain and the Channel Isles consisted of 7 national brewers, 88 independent brewers and 5 home brewers for sale (that is a 'home brewer' who sells his beer to the general public and not just for home consumption). Seventy per cent of our beer is supplied by the nationally distributing companies. The change in the industry has been from home to wholesale brewing and a concentration of wholesale brewers brought about by amalgamations and takeovers. (Maltsters have also been affected.)

Predictions have been made that another ten years or so could see the eclipse of the regional independent brewer and the supply of all beer vested in the hands of a few large combines. The Monopolies and Mergers Act of 1965 defines a monopoly as being over one-third of the market, so in theory it would be possible to end up with three giant combines entrusted with the job of satisfying the thirst and controlling the drinking habits of every beer drinker in the country.

Amalgamations and takeovers have been a feature of the brewer's world for a very long time, and the end of the line has almost been reached. Regional brewers are spread fairly evenly over the country, although there are some quite large gaps which they no longer penetrate. Even in areas where there are local brewers still operating their pubs are not always easy to find (without the information in this book) because they may own only a few and they may be up side roads. It is upon the regional beers to a large extent that the beer drinker has to depend for a drink of character and a wide variety of palate (flavour).

There have been four principal reasons for takeovers in the brewing industry. Public companies are very exposed to the danger of a takeover unless the shares are securely held and cannot easily be bought by outside interests. Then there is the straightforward sale of a family concern, and who can blame the owner if he is offered the prospect of riches? Quite a common reason for small breweries having to sell out has been the death of a member of the family and the consequent payment of death duties to the government which could not be paid without selling the business. In addition there were the breweries which sold out in the early fifties and other times when the beer business was not prospering as it is today. It is doubtful if a takeover has ever occurred because of inferior beer—perhaps lack of support, but that is quite a different thing and usually inspired by the false notion that beer from afar or beer that is advertised must be better.

What is of importance here is how the creation of the giant dinosaurs in industry affects the drinking man, because there is little doubt that the concentration of the brewing business, with its important place in our social life, affects the consumer more than amalgamations in some other businesses.

Rationalisation is a word which is heard and read quite commonly nowadays, not least in the brewing world. It is defined as a reorganisation so as to avoid waste, and to the beer drinker it means the loss of local, and perhaps favourite, beers when a brewery is taken over. Points of production have been rationalised and there are numerous derelict breweries all over the country. This, of course, has brought about a diminution of choice and a trend towards standardisation with sterile beers which can be delivered in bulk by tankers over long distances.

Rationalisation has not been restricted to beers and breweries. Many pubs have been sold because they have not been economic ventures in the sense that realisation of the capital by sale has been more profitable than continuing to sell a steady but perhaps relatively small amount of beer. This is sound economic sense but very unfortunate for many country people whose villages have become 'dry' and their social life changed. Some towns have had so many pubs in the past that, with rising costs, it has become impossible for them all to provide a living. There have also been instances where a brewer, via the takeover trail, has become the owner of all the pubs (perhaps two or three which were previously each owned by different brewers) in a village. By means of a restrictive covenant in the sale of two of the houses preventing their further use as pubs, any possible competition has been avoided at the same time as reaping the profits from the sales. Fortunately this practice is now discouraged as a result of its having being taken up in Parliament. Pubs in developed areas have also been lost, but most towns are still well supplied with drinking outlets and it is the country areas which have been affected most by the changes.

The elimination of competition is an inevitable feature brought about by a concentration of industry. In some towns there is still a healthy variety of different brewers' outlets, and for the fortunate beer drinker there is no chance of becoming bored by a lack of choice. One's favourite brew tastes all the better for an occasional sip around other brews. Other towns, in fact some large areas of countryside, are less lucky and may be virtually monopolised by a brewer who has gobbled up all the other breweries in that area. Here the man with a discriminating thirst must take what is offered or travel long distances in search of other brewers' pubs—and many beer drinkers all over the country are now doing just that.

Lack of competition tends towards less stabilised prices, but there are a number of reasons for the higher price of beer today other than rising costs in general. Whereas in the past pubs were regarded essentially as outlets for a brewer's products, they are now looked upon primarily as capital investments from which a high return is demanded. A large sum is involved in tied-up capital when several thousand pubs are owned. Then, with nationally distributed beers, advertising on a national scale has become a regular and expensive feature of the brewing scene, usually aimed at convincing the consumer, who pays in the end, that one or other of the national beers is the best. The trend towards keg and container beers has also tended towards higher prices because of the expensive additional equipment—such as is needed for chilling, filtering and pasteurising—required in their production.

A fairly frequent disturbance in recent years has been the beer famine caused by industrial disputes at the brewery which has more widespread effects when it is a very large brewery. With the concentration of points of production this is an ever-increasing risk.

Throughout the whole country there is an enormous variety of beers with different flavours to be enjoyed by the adventurous beer drinker, but it is subject to continual erosion. Nationally distributed beers tend to be very similar and it has been said that people now like their beer to have the same palate in whatever part of the country they may be drinking. As Britons have not yet become a race with no powers of discrimination it is unlikely to be a true assessment but rather a statement to match the present trends.

Many beers have become sweeter and it has been said that it is in response to public demand. However, there is still a very strong support for the good bitter, well-hopped, and what can best be described as 'beery' beers. It would be scientifically impossible for the human race to evolve new taste buds in the space of one generation and the simple fact is that some people have a sweeter tooth than others. A sweeter beer may well increase the scope of the market because the fairer sex generally has a sweeter tooth. A lemonade-type of beer is popular with people who may not otherwise have drunk beer at all. 'Beery' beers have become less common in recent years, to the consternation of beer drinkers of all age groups.

There have been many changes in pubs themselves, sometimes to the good, and brewers of all sizes have spent large sums on what they regard as improvements in comfort and amenities. Catering facilities are now much more common, and many prefer to eat in a pub rather than in a more formal restaurant or cafe. The pub has always been a great social centre and it is a pity that many country pubs have disappeared (often leaving whole villages dry), while in some instances the public bar, with its informal atmosphere, has been lost. In many cases brewers' signs have become more conspicuous than the name of the pub itself, which is not always pleasing to the eye.

Many brewers now produce their own lager, and a very refreshing drink it is for the summer months, as it should always be served at a lower temperature than beer. The 'lager revolution' really started in Scotland (although lager was first brewed many years ago in England, as already explained) and has now spread to south of the border.

True draught beers have had to make way to some extent for the keg beers, which in some instances have replaced them. In Scotland draught beers have become scarce and detective work is needed to find them (which is not difficult with the aid of this

Page 67 (*above*) Fermenting vats at the Dorchester brewery; (*below*) traditional wooden casks being filled with draught beer at the same brewery

Page 68 (*above left*) Hop cone ready for picking; (*above right*) hop stringing being cut at harvesting at the Guinness hop farms; (*below*) three traditional oast houses, where the hops are dried, at the Guinness hop farms, Bodiam

book), and one brewer in the south has abandoned them altogether. They are beers of great character and variety and many brewers pride themselves on their draught beers with good reason. It would be a severe loss if they should disappear under the false banner of progress or rationalisation.

There is the trend towards beer dispensed by means of CO_2 gas, for which many people have an ardent dislike because of its effect on the beer's taste. That it does make a difference has been shown by tasting tests.

What about the future? It would certainly be good for the industry if the small end of the brewing world was allowed to go about its business without the perpetual fear of takeover and consequent redundancies. That would be good for the consumer too, who could continue to look forward to a reasonable choice. The Common Market is another question. Regulations have been mentioned which do not entirely match with the traditional methods of brewing British beer, and perhaps the fear most often voiced is whether the use of seedless hops will result in the loss of top-fermented beers. This is unlikely, because they can be brewed with either seeded or seedless hops (although seedless hops are said to give a more delicate flavour and may not have the full, fruity flavour of some seeded varieties), while as already mentioned, seedless hops could not be established in the British hop-growing countryside because of the abundance of wild hops in the hedgerows.

One result of the industry's concentration and the consequent diminishing choice and loss of favourite beers has been the formation of a number of societies whose objective is to look after the interests of the consumer. One such society has received publicity from local press and is called CAMRA—the Campaign for Real Ale. It was formed in 1971 and has a large membership which is drawn partly from the brewing industry itself. A guide to several hundred pubs which serve good draught beer, not artificially carbonated, has been produced and a more comprehensive edition is planned.

In recent years many small breweries that still produce natural beers have been flourishing, with many customers willing to travel miles to find beers of character, and some breweries that had closed have even been reopened. Selby Brewery recommenced brewing after a gap of nearly twenty years (see p 218) and Traquair House Ale was reborn in the mid-sixties after 200 years (p 78), so why not others in the future? It is certainly possible and a very exciting prospect.

CHAPTER 6

Home-Brewed Houses

Many years ago nearly every private citizen brewed his own beer, which at that time was a lot safer to drink than water, and even up to the early nineteenth century about half the brewing in England was done privately. It was during the Middle Ages that the 'common brewer'—who brewed beer for any alehouse that did not brew its own—appeared on the scene. It may not be generally known that there are still a number of public houses in existence that brew their own beer on the premises for sale to the public.

Up to about the sixteenth century, nearly every house had its own home brewer and very often the housewife herself was not only the cook and bottle-washer but the head brewer as well. She was the brewster, which was the name for a female brewer. Probably less than 20 per cent of beer brewed at that time was brewed by alehouse-keepers in their own alehouses for sale to the public. It was a natural process of evolution that bigger (and perhaps better) alehouse keepers should appear on the scene who brewed not only for their own requirements but also for other alehouse-keepers. These were the common brewers, and they filled a very important niche in society because in those days brewing was a very hit-or-miss occupation, lacking the benefits of the scientific knowledge and control of the present day. It only wanted a spell of hot weather for the beer to go 'off', or cold days for the fermentation to be difficult to start, or for some unwanted bug-like intruders to upset the fermentation. It must have been a very chancy business, especially before hops with their preservative powers appeared on the scene. Then, perhaps, there were supply problems, so with one thing and another it would have been a relief to the alehouse-keeper to know that supplies could still be ensured should there be an emergency.

In those days the public was well catered for in the matter of alehouses, inns or taverns, as it is known that a population of under four million was served by about 20,000 of these drinking dens. This works out at one pub for every 200 or less members of the public—men, women and children—which was not too bad considering that most of the brewing was done privately. Domestic brewing for home consumption is certainly becoming very popular today, but it is on nothing like the scale of the Middle Ages; and today there would be scarcely one pub to nearly 1,000 citizens.

The number of home-brewed houses has declined very rapidly over the years and it is fortunate that today there are still five establishments brewing beer on the premises for sale to the public. This is a very small proportion when it is considered that in the early eighteenth century half of all beer brewed was in home-brewed houses. The numbers have gradually diminished up to the present day and in the last year or two several home-brewed houses have ceased brewing for one reason or another. For instance the Druids Head at Coseley near Wolverhampton in the Black Country ceased brewing in 1971 because the landlord and brewer Mr Jack Flavell unfortunately died. It continued to supply a local brew—JPS Bitter—for a time until it was eventually developed out of existence altogether. Then there was the Friary Hotel in Derby which gave up in the same year needing some repairs or renovation to the equipment. Mr Clayton of the Nag's Head at Belper just north of Derby also ceased brewing his own beer recently, and it is certain that many tipplers would be delighted if these two decided to recommence operations. The most recent loss to the home brew addict was Mr Herbert North of the Britannia Inn at Loughborough. Mr North died early on Sunday morning 28 May 1972 from an illness—he was nearly 65—but right up to the last he was making his home brew and he had completed his normal rounds with his latest brew only a few hours previously. Mr North's brother, Mr Harry North, has taken over the licence for the time being, but the draught beer comes from outside and the regular customers 'hooked' on home brew miss the 'Best' and 'Mild' which Mr North used to brew. It is interesting to trace the origin of this home-brewed house, and Mr Harry North has kindly supplied a few details.

It all started with Mr North's father at the start of the century. He was the brewer for a local brewery and he travelled around the district on his bicycle as a freelance brewer to similar houses brewing their own beer. During World War I he took a house of his own (the Queen's Head in Barrow St) which became redundant in 1923, by which time the North family had moved into the Britannia Inn; but outside brewing came to an end with the free houses being swallowed up by the local breweries. When father and mother North died in 1940, Herbert took over the licence and had been brewing ever since. Mr North used no sugar—only malt and hops—in his home brew, and his maltster has since stated that he was able to get more from his malt than anyone he knew. The whole family of two sisters and four brothers contributed towards the success of the North home brew which kept its head—a natural one—right down to the last swallow and it was never necessary to blow the beer up with gas or to advertise. In fact the family boasted with some justification that they never lost a customer. So a family's tradition of brewing has sadly come to an end.

The Midlands have always been richly provided with home-brewed houses and all of the most recent ones to cease operations have come from this region. Three of the remaining five are from the Midlands, the other two being in Cornwall and Scotland. Apologies are offered to any home-brewed house still brewing but not mentioned here and also congratulations on preserving the secret from a well-trained sniffer-out of such establishments. The five houses are as follows:

All Nations Inn, Coalport Rd, Madeley, Telford, Shropshire. The licensee is W.H. Lewis. Mrs Lewis does all the brewing and has done so for the last thirty-eight years, since the licence of this pub was acquired. Once a week, when most good citizens are in the depths of their slumber, Mrs Lewis rises in the small hours and commences operations at 3 am. It is not for another twelve hours or so that she has finished brewing, including clearing up. Mrs Lewis brews in a building behind the pub and there can be seen the boiler and two large vats, one for cooling and one for fermenting. The vats each hold about 260 gallons and Mrs Lewis used to move the liquor from one vat to the next by means of a hand ladle. She says it kept her fit and she must have been very adept at this laborious operation as she did it in only a quarter of an hour. Now the operation is more mechanised with a new boiler and an electric pump. The home brew at the All Nations Inn is a Midland-style light mild, and very palatable.

The Blue Anchor Inn, Coinagehall St, Helston, Cornwall. The host at this house is Mr Geoffrey Richards and he represents the third generation of his family to hold a licence to brew here. It was only by chance that Mr Richards' grandfather became the brewer at the Blue Anchor when he called there one hundred or more years ago to quench his thirst. The inn was being auctioned at that very time and place, and as there had been no takers Mr Richards made his bid and found himself the new owner.

But the history of the Blue Anchor goes back 600 years to 1400 when it was a Monk's Rest, where the monks had a brief respite from the rigours of their monastic life. Here they brewed beer, and no doubt drank it while they rested in peace and contemplation.

About 300 years later the Monk's Rest fell into disuse and it became an inn; larger brewing equipment was installed together with a skittle alley. Pint measures were kid's stuff in those days and it was the custom to take beer by the gallon down to the skittle alley, and at 1s 4d a gallon it must have been good value. The public bar was also used to pay the weekly wages of the tin miners, and it requires little imagination to visualise the subsequent beer-swilling, drunken brawls and bawdy-song singing. To the colourful history of this ancient inn can be added stories of a murder and two suicides. The murdered man was Mr James the landlord who was accidentally stabbed when intervening in a brawl in the public bar in 1790. One of the suicides hanged himself in the skittle alley and the other threw himself down a well which is still at the back of the inn. Spingo—in two strengths—is the name of the beer at the Blue Anchor Inn. It was introduced by Mr Richards' father after World War I, no doubt to 'build up the men of Helston after their fight and to strengthen their sons for the next one'. Spingo has a slight cloud of yeast and the modern visual drinker would surely hand it back to the landlord if it was in a more modern pub. But the Spingo addicts of Helston and others from far afield drink it cheerfully, knowing that their pint is the better for it. Malt and hops are the ingredients, and after mashing and boiling Spingo is allowed to ferment in barrels in the cellar for about two weeks. Mr Richards also has a special brew up his sleeve for Christmas and Easter.

Mrs Pardoe's Old Swan Brewery, Halesowen Road, Netherton, Dudley, six miles south-east of Wolverhampton. The Old Swan is in the main street of Netherton, and passed into the Pardoe family forty years ago, although there was brewing there many years before that. Mrs Pardoe is an expert at her craft and she can tell by a look and a sniff whether her latest brew is up to her high standard. There is also another pub owned by the family and which supplies the brew from the Old Swan. This is at Dudley and can be found by coming out of the town with Julia Hanson's brewery on the right then turning right near the cemetery into Holland Street which is off Wellington Road. This is a modern pub called the White Swan.

Mrs Pardoe's agreeable home-brewed ale is a bitter which lies, in palate, about midway between a bitter and a mild.

Three Tuns Brewery, Bishop's Castle, Shropshire, Bishop's Castle is a peaceful country town in the rolling Border countryside, and the casual passer-by would be unlikely to guess that it is the home of one of the few home-brewed houses remaining. The licensee, proprietor and brewer is Mr John C.E. Roberts. The brew house situated at the back of the inn's car park is an impressive building and was installed in 1888 by the grandfather of the present licensee. It operates, like the traditional tower breweries, on gravity. The brew starts at the highest level in the mash tun from which it progresses to the copper for boiling, then to the hop-back, cooler, fermenting vessels, and eventually into wooden or metal casks where it is dry hopped.

Mr Roberts brews a draught mild and draught XXX which is a well-flavoured bitter with the smack of hops from the nearby West Midland hopyards. They used to do their own malting at the Three Tuns up to 1935 when Mr Roberts' father gave it up. Now the malt comes from Yorkshire or East Anglia.

There was a time when the Three Tuns supplied its draught beer to a number of other pubs in the district but this is not so any more, and a visit to the Three Tuns itself is necessary—and worthwhile—in order to taste Mr Roberts' traditional brew.

Traquair House, Innerleithen, Peebles-shire, Scotland. This picturesque, massive but homely grey-walled building is said to be Scotland's oldest inhabited house, dating back to the twelfth century. It lies on the road to St Mary's Loch close by Innerleithen, which is on the main Edinburgh—Peebles—Galashiels road. It is a house alive with ancient history but it also has something of interest to the searcher for good or unusual beer—the Traquair House Ale. That this should be so may seem at first a little bizarre; but when it is remembered that brewing was practised at many of the great houses in the past it is surprising that not more of the stately homes have old brew-houses still in existence. In fact there are very few apart from Charlecote Park in Warwickshire and Shibden Hall near Halifax, neither of which is in working order. Traquair House, until some years ago, was a stately home famous for its architecture, its treasures, and its Bear Gates, which were closed after Bonnie Prince Charlie passed through them and are never to be opened until a Stuart king comes to the throne. Now it has become connected with the art of brewing because P. Maxwell Stuart, the 20th Laird of Traquair, discovered the old brew house complete with brewing utensils during a massive spring-cleaning operation. Mr Maxwell Stuart did better than that because he put the 200-years-old utensils into working order and in 1965 recommenced operations—after a gap of some two centuries. There was a brewery at Traquair when Mary Queen of Scots visited there in 1566 and it could have been that Bonnie Prince Charlie tasted the ale on his visit to the house in 1745.

The Belhaven Brewery at Dunbar (no 23) provided the technical aid and also the facilities for bottling the ale in two sizes of bottle, all bottles being individually numbered. Each brew produces about 115 gallons of strong ale with an original gravity of about 1080, and barley, malt and hops are the only materials used. Traquair House Ale is brewed three or four times a year and the fifteenth brew since the brew house was reopened took place in mid-1972. Up to this time nearly 20,000 half-pint bottles had been produced. Like vintage wines, but to a lesser degree, there are subtle differences between brews, which may vary in strength, sharpness and sweetness, but all seem to improve with age up to about four years and maybe much longer.

The ale can be obtained, of course, at Traquair House, but it is also available in a number of other places. These include: Young & Saunders Ltd, Queensferry St, Edinburgh; Houston House Hotel, Broxburn, near Edinburgh; Gordon Arms Hotel, Yarrow; Park Hotel, Peebles; Traquair Arms Hotel, Innerleithen; Old Mill Inn, Blyth Bridge, Peeblesshire; Howgate Inn, Howgate, to the south of Edinburgh; Marchbank Hotel, Balerno, near Edinburgh; and Old Eagle Inn, Howard St, Glasgow. In London it is not now at Parke's Restaurant; it can now be obtained at The Cock and Rabbit at the Lee, near Great Missenden, Bucks. As production increases it is hoped to extend the number of inns and hotels selling the ale in Scotland and to expand to the north of England.

Traquair, with its many other interests apart from the ale, is open to the public from 1 July to 30 September daily except Fridays from 2 pm to 5.30 pm and every Sunday from 14 May to 24 September, and parties can be arranged at other times.

These five houses not only reach back into past

history and preserve in a unique manner an earlier way of life; they also brew high-quality beers with character which have a way of growing on one. Both are good reasons for their preservation—fortunately there is little to fear through lack of patronage, because there are plenty of discerning drinkers still around. It would be easy to imagine the success of a new home-brewed house in another part of the country—especially in this era of standardisation. If there is any property developer with vision, looking for a sound investment, reading this, he could do worse than give it some thought—the equipment can still be obtained.

CHAPTER 7

The Regional (Independent) Brewers

All the brewery companies listed in this section are regional in that they supply a limited area of the country and their beers cannot be obtained on a national scale. They are also independent in that they brew their own beers and operate independently from other brewers. In some cases the owner may be another company outside the brewing business (and so not strictly independent), while in some other instances another large company—possibly brewing—may have a stake. With these qualifications, the description is accurate and practical from the consumer's point of view. Some independent brewers may regretfully disappear by being taken over in the future, but although minor changes are inevitable it can reasonably be predicted that the information given here will remain substantially up-to-date and of practical value for quite a number of years.

The information has been obtained by personal observation and has then been checked with the companies concerned to eliminate possible inaccuracies. Virtually all draught beers and many of the bottled beers have been sampled. In one instance it was not possible to make a final check because communication could not be established and letters were unanswered; in some other cases it was very difficult to establish communication. Some brewers have been very secretive about their activities, which is not altogether surprising because they receive so many requests for information and other things, and on occasions have had bad publicity—sometimes mis-informed and inaccurate. However it could be that this has resulted for the very reason of their secrecy and unwillingness to divulge facts more freely. Some companies are even reluctant to give the whereabouts of their pubs—most necessary information for the enthusiastic supporter of that firm's brew, yet some-times denied him. Most companies were extremely co-operative and helpful in every way.

The piece on each brewery company is as practical as possible with the information available and starts with a catch-phrase or slogan most often associated with that particular concern. The 'Address' paragraph may include reference to any features of interest about the town or locality and the brewery itself. Then under 'Recognition' is a description of the signs to look out for on the pubs. This is followed by 'Tied houses' where the object has been to make it as easy as possible to locate the pubs without resorting to long lists of pubs' names which are not always available and would be extremely lengthy in some cases. Where it would be difficult to find a pub, such as where there are only a few in a large town, or where a pub is a long way outside the main trading area, the name of the street to look for or the pub's name has been given. Sometimes the trading area has been very broadly defined and limits given within which it is not difficult to locate some of the pubs.

With other companies the area is less clearly defined and a little more detective work is needed—which can be quite entertaining if one is not in a violent hurry. There is usually a reference to the free trade.

The beers themselves have been listed under draught, keg and bottled. Reference is also made to container (tank) beers and beer in cans. Draught bitters have been classified as far as possible, but of course tastes and opinions are very variable and nothing quite replaces personal experience. Within the category of 'well-hopped beer' there is a whole variety of different tastes depending on the kind of hops and many other things. A 'well-balanced beer' does not necessarily mean a lack of flavour but rather one where no flavour is outstanding or at the expense of another. Some draught beers are distinctly 'malty' and others 'nutty'. Some are extremely sweet and lack the characteristic taste of beer.

It would be impossible to define satisfactorily the whole range of barley wines and other bottled beers with their variety of subtle flavours, and as preferences are so individual it is a case of trying as many as possible. The main thing is to know just what is available. The first excursion into a pub of an unfamiliar brewer can be quite bewildering to the thirsty traveller who may give a hurried order for a drink he does not really want, without prior knowledge of the beers available.

Finally the dispensing systems for the draught beers to be found in each brewer's pubs are given.

Heavitree Brewery Ltd, Heavitree, Exeter, with pubs in and around Exeter is independent but no longer brews. The beers for its pubs (which have Heavitree signs) are obtained from Whitbread & Co. Ltd. Many people regretted the loss of Heavitree's own excellent beers, but as they are no more, the company is not listed.

Bottled beers which have been brewed for various multiple trading concerns are not listed, but they are usually normal pale or brown ales or a few others.

The companies are in alphabetical order and all have numbers which refer to the numbers on the map on page 89. Consequently it is simple to find out which brewers are covering any particular area of the country - taking into account that the extent of the area covered may be large and within a wide circle or only in the immediate vicinity of the number on the map.

The Regional (Independent) Breweries of Great Britain and the Channel Islands

Note The numbers relate
to the numbers on the map (p. 89)

1. Adnams & Co Ltd, Southwold, Suffolk
2. Ann Street Brewery Co Ltd, St Helier, Jersey, Channel Islands
3. J. Arkell & Sons Ltd, Swindon, Wilts
4. L.C. Arkell, Donnington Brewery, Stow-on-the-Wold, Gloucestershire
5. George Bateman & Sons Ltd, Wainfleet, Skegness, Lincs
6. Daniel Batham & Son Ltd, Brierley Hill, Staffs
7. Beard & Co (Lewes) Ltd, Lewes, Sussex
8. Boddingtons' Breweries Ltd, Manchester, Lancs
9. Border Breweries (Wrexham) Ltd, Wrexham, North Wales
10. S.A. Brain & Co Ltd, Cardiff, South Wales
11. W.H. Brakspear & Sons Ltd, Henley-on-Thames, Oxfordshire
12. Matthew Brown & Co Ltd, Blackburn, Lancs
13. Buckley's Brewery Ltd, Llanelli, Carmarthen, South Wales
14. Burt & Co, Ventnor, Isle of Wight
15. Burtonwood Brewery Co (Forshaws) Ltd, Burtonwood, Warrington, Lancs
16. J.W. Cameron & Co. Ltd, Hartlepool, Co Durham
17. Carlisle and District State Management Scheme, Cumberland
18. Castletown Brewery Ltd, Castletown, Isle of Man
19. G.E. Cook & Sons Ltd, Halstead, Essex

20. W.M. Darley Ltd, Thorne, Doncaster, Yorks
21. Davenports' C.B. & Brewery (Holdings) Ltd, Birmingham, Warwickshire
22. J.A. Devenish & Co Ltd, Weymouth, Dorset
23. Dudgeon & Co Ltd, Dunbar, East Lothian, Scotland
24. Eldridge, Pope & Co Ltd, Dorchester, Dorset
25. Elgood & Sons Ltd, Wisbech, Cambs
26. Everards Brewery Ltd, Leicester
27. The Felinfoel Brewery Co Ltd, Felinfoel, Llanelli, South Wales
28. Fuller, Smith & Turner Ltd, Chiswick, London
29. George Gale & Co Ltd, Horndean, Portsmouth, Hants
30. Gibbs, Mew & Co Ltd, Salisbury, Wilts
31. Gray & Sons (Brewers) Ltd, Chelmsford, Essex
32. Greenall, Whitley & Co Ltd, Warrington, Lancs
33a. Greene, King & Sons Ltd, Bury St Edmunds, Suffolk
33b. Greene, King (Biggleswade) Ltd,
33c. Rayment & Co Ltd, Furneux Pelham, Buntingford, Herts
34. The Guernsey Brewery Co (1920) Ltd, St Peter Port, Guernsey
35. Hall & Woodhouse Ltd, Blandford Forum, Dorset
36. Hardys and Hansons Ltd, Kimberley, Nottingham
37. Hartleys' (Ulverston) Ltd, Ulverston, Lancs
38. Harvey & Son (Lewes) Ltd, Lewes, Sussex
39. Higsons Brewery Ltd, Liverpool, Lancs
40. Holden's Brewery Ltd, Woodsetten, Dudley, Worcs
41. Joseph Holt Ltd, Cheetham, Manchester, Lancs
42. Home Brewery Co Ltd, Daybrook, Notts

43. Hook Norton Brewery Co Ltd, Hook Norton, Banbury, Oxfordshire
44. T. Hoskins Ltd, Leicester
45. The Hull Brewery Co Ltd, Hull, Yorks
46. Hydes' Anvil Brewery Ltd, Manchester, Lancs
47. Jennings Brothers Ltd, Cockermouth, Cumberland
48. JPS Breweries Ltd, Brierley Hill, Staffs
49. King & Barnes Ltd, Horsham, Sussex
50. J.W. Lees & Co (Brewers) Ltd, Middleton Junction, Manchester, Lancs
51. Maclay & Co Ltd, Alloa, Clackmannanshire, Scotland
52. McMullen & Sons Ltd, Hertford, Herts
53. Mansfield Brewery Co Ltd, Mansfield, Notts
54. Marston, Thompson & Evershed Ltd, Burton-upon-Trent, Staffs
55. Melbourns Brewery Ltd, Stamford, Lincs
56. Mitchells of Lancaster (Brewers) Ltd, Lancaster, Lancs
57. Morland & Co Ltd, Abingdon, Berks
58. Morrell's Brewery Ltd, Oxford
59. The Northern Clubs' Federation Brewery Ltd, Newcastle-upon-Tyne
60. Okell & Sons Ltd, Douglas, Isle of Man
61. Oldham Brewery Co Ltd, Oldham, Lancs
62. Paine & Co Ltd, St Neots, Hunts
63. J.C. & R.H. Palmer, Bridport, Dorset
64. Randalls Brewery Ltd, St Helier, Jersey, Channel Islands
65. R.W. Randall Ltd, St Peter Port, Guernsey, Channel Islands
66. T.D. Ridley & Sons Ltd, Chelmsford, Essex
67. Frederic Robinson Ltd, Stockport, Cheshire
68. G. Ruddle & Co Ltd, Langham, Oakham, Rutland

69. St Austell Brewery Co Ltd, St Austell, Cornwall
70. Selby (Middlebrough) Brewery Ltd, Selby, Yorks
71. Shepherd Neame Ltd, Faversham, Kent
72. James Shipstone & Sons Ltd, New Basford, Nottingham
73. Samuel Smith Old Brewery (Tadcaster) Ltd, Tadcaster, Yorks
74. South Wales and Monmouthshire United Clubs Brewery Co Ltd, Pontyclun, Glamorganshire
75. Timothy Taylor & Co Ltd, Keighley, Yorks
76. T. & R. Theakston Ltd, Masham, Ripon, Yorks
77. Daniel Thwaites & Co Ltd, Blackburn, Lancs
78. Tollemache & Cobbold Breweries Ltd, Ipswich, Suffolk
79. Truman Ltd, London
80a. Vaux and Associated Breweries Ltd, Sunderland, Co Durham
80b. Thos. Usher & Son Ltd, and Caledonian Brewery, Edinburgh
81. Wadworth & Co Ltd, Devizes, Wilts
82. S.H. Ward & Co Ltd, Sheffield, Yorks
83. Charles Wells Ltd, Bedford, Beds
84. The Wolverhampton & Dudley Breweries Ltd, Wolverhampton, Staffs
85. Workington Brewery Co Ltd, Workington, Cumberland
86. Yates & Jackson Ltd, Lancaster, Lancs
87. Yorkshire Clubs' Brewery Ltd, Huntington, York
88. Young & Co's Brewery Ltd, Wandsworth, London

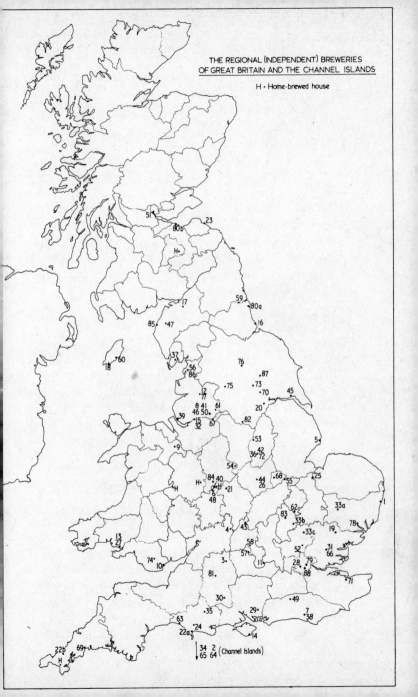

THE REGIONAL (INDEPENDENT) BREWERIES
OF GREAT BRITAIN AND THE CHANNEL ISLANDS

H • Home-brewed house

34 2
65 64 (Channel Islands)

1   ADNAMS & CO LTD

'Southwold Ales'

ADDRESS

Sole Bay Brewery, Southwold, Suffolk. Tel 2424.

Southwold is a pleasant old town and seaside resort with a harbour at the mouth of the river Blyth on the Suffolk coast. Just to the south is the coastal village of Dunwich (which was mostly swept away by the sea) and further on the bird sanctuary at Minsmere.

In addition to their normal transport, Adnams deliver their ales by horse and dray within a five-mile radius of Southwold and for this purpose keep a team of four grey Percherons.

RECOGNITION

Usually 'Adnams' is writte in large letters on the pub wall or 'Adnams Southwold Ales' or close variations. There may also be a black plaque by the door with 'Adnams Southwold Ales' written in gold letters. The trade mark is 'Southwold Jack' who is a four-teenth-century knight in armour striking a bell with his sword; he can be seen in Southwold church.

TIED HOUSES

There are just under 70 of these and they are mainly within a compact area in East Suffolk, many of them pleasant country inns and some of them residential. The trading area is mostly contained within a line starting at Orford on the coast north-east of Felixstowe, then travelling inland through Butley, Wickham Market, Brandeston, and as far as Eye near the Norwich-Ipswich road, then north-east to Harleston, Bungay, Geldeston and Lowestoft (eg Prince Albert).

Outside this imaginary line there are Adnams houses at Martlesham near Ipswich, at Ipswich itself (Greyhound, Rose & Crown), Felixstowe (Little Ships Hotel) and Colchester (Castle Hotel).

There is a flourishing free trade extending well into Norfolk, also Essex and Cambridgeshire. A separate company, the Sole Bay Hotel Co, looks after the residential houses. Norfolk outlets which sell Adnams ales are as follows: Wherry, Norwich; Maids Head, Norwich; Royal Hotel, Norwich; Park Hotel, Diss; Hare & Hounds, Hempstead; Salad Bowl Restaurant, Cromer; Ingoldisthorpe Manor Hotel, Ingoldisthorpe; Maltings Hotel, Weybourne; St Marys Country Club, Happisburgh; Buckinghamshire Arms and Blickling Arms, Blickling; Manor Hotel, Blakeney; Red Lion Hotel, Cromer; Sutton Staithe Hotel & Country Club, Stalham; Black Horse and Hare & Hounds, Castle Rising; Overstrand Court Hotel, Overstrand; Three Horseshoes, Titchwell; The Alex Club, Cromer; Links Hotel. West Runton; Kings Head, Letheringsett; Manor Grill, Happisburgh; Haig Club, Mundesley; United Services Club, Blakeney; Royal Cromer Golf Club.

BEERS

Draught	Bitter. A very distinctive flavoured and popular draught bitter.
	Mild. A dark mild.
	Strong Ale. An old ale for the winter.
Keg	Keg Bitter. Mainly in the free trade.
Bottled	Champion Pale Ale.
	Fishermans Strong.
	Broadside.
	These two are strong pale ales.

Tally Ho. A barley wine in nips. It is also
on draught at Christmas time.

Nut Brown Ale. Medium sweet.

Draught beers are dispensed by manual bar pumps,
direct from the cask, or in some cases by top pressure
or electric pumps.

2   ANN STREET BREWERY CO LTD

'The Beers that make Jersey famous'
'Jersey's own brew'

ADDRESS

57 Ann Street, St Helier, Jersey, Channel Islands. Tel
C 31561.

The stockholders in the Ann Street Brewery Company are almost entirely from Jersey and the States
of Jersey has substantial holdings, the dividends from
which are given to two charities. All raw materials for
brewing are imported from Britain. Licensing laws in
the island are very relaxed, and the pubs are open
from 9 am until 11 pm in summer, and 9 am until 10
pm in the winter. Bar staff work on a shift system.

RECOGNITION

'Mary Ann Pale Ale' is often written in large letters
on the wall of the pub; or 'This is a Mary Ann house'
with an illuminated hanging sign with a yellow shield
and crossed daggers, chosen as being synonymous
with quality and value. The house colours are blue
and white and the yellow shield is being replaced by a
blue one.

TIED HOUSES

There are 50 of these and they include the oldest pub in Jersey, the Foresters Arms at Beaumont. The majority of the trade is free and Mary Ann beers can be drunk in every parish on the island. In addition, Mary Ann products are sold in a majority of the public houses which are owned by local wine merchants.

BEERS

Keg	Best Bitter. Quite a well hopped keg bitter.
	Extra Special Bitter. This is stronger and sweeter than the BB and is claimed to be the strongest beer in keg in the UK
Bottled	Mary Ann Pale Ale.
	Mary Ann Special. A strong pale ale which has been introduced only recently.
	Mary Ann Brown Ale. Medium sweet.
	Mary Ann Stout. A dry stout.

Harp Lager and Watneys Red are kegged at the brewery, and Double Diamond, Guinness, Mackeson Stout, Mann's Brown, Skol Lager, and Worthington E are bottled. Draught guinness is sold in the pubs. Draught beers are dispensed by top pressure.

3   J. ARKELL & SONS LTD

'Arkell's Ales'

ADDRESS

Kingsdown Brewery, Upper Stratton, Swindon, Wilts.

Tel Stratton St Margaret 3026.

Upper Stratton is a north-eastern suburb of Swindon, a town famous for its railway engineering and 29 miles south-west of Oxford.

RECOGNITION

'Arkell's', or 'Arkell's Ales' or 'Arkell's Fine Ales' is written on the inn sign or the outside wall of the pub. The letters are usually in blue or red, but also sometimes green or white. The house sign—to be seen on a plaque on the pub wall—is a Noah's Ark with an embossed letter 'L'.

TIED HOUSES

33 of the 62 licensed houses are in Swindon and its suburbs and in the villages within a radius of five miles or so. But the outer circle of good 'Arkell' drinking runs further afield through Cirencester (Plume of Feathers, Golden Cross, Brewers Arms, Talbot), Fairford, Lechlade, Faringdon (in Ferndale Street), Lambourne, Aldbourne, Hilmarton, Kemble and back to Cirencester. There is some free trade within a fifteen-mile radius.

BEERS

Draught   Bitter. A draught bitter with a pleasant nutty flavour.

BBB. 'Best Bitter Beer' and stronger than the ordinary bitter.

Keg   Keg Bitter. This is the BBB chilled and filtered but not pasteurised. It is not available in all houses as the local demand is satisfied by the Bitter or the BBB.

Bottled   Pale Ale. Not unlike the bitter in flavour. BBB. A strong pale ale. Strong Ale. Stronger than the BBB. Brown Ale.

Draught beers are dispensed mostly by top pressure. A few houses still have bar pumps or serve direct from the cask.

4 L.C. ARKELL—DONNINGTON BREWERY

'Donnington Ales'

ADDRESS

Donnington Brewery, Stow-on-the-Wold, Gloucestershire. Tel 603.

Stow-on-the-Wold lies at a junction of six roads in the north-eastern Cotswolds, and 21 miles to the south of Stratford-on-Avon.

The brewery is situated in peaceful, rural surroundings just to the south of the road to Broadway and towards Condicote. It even has its name on a signpost pointing the way to a fold in the hills which encloses the Cotswold-stone brewery, a millpond alive with waterfowl, many of them exotic, and a millstream full of trout.

RECOGNITION

Black inn-signs with 'Donnington Ales' written in white letters.

TIED HOUSES

There are 17 of these which are situated in very pleasant surroundings in the rolling countryside. There is a Donnington house at Stow itself (Queens Head) and just to the north in Broadwell, Ganborough and Longborough. To the south-west of Stow the black sign can be seen at Lower Swell, Naunton, Guiting Power; to the west at Kineton and Ford; and up towards Broadway at Snowshill. The outer circle of Donnington drinking runs through Willersey (north of Broadway), Moreton-in-Marsh (Black Bear), Little Compton, Fifield (south of Stow on the Burford road), Great Barrington (to the west of Burford), Winchcombe (Bell Inn) and Stanton which is further north-east towards Broadway.

BEERS

Draught   BB. A well balanced draught bitter with a smack of hops.
SBA. Stronger and a little sweeter.
XXX Mild. A dark mild.

Bottled   Light Ale. The BB in bottle.
Double Donn. The SBA in bottle.
Brown Ale. The XXX in bottle.

Draught beers are dispensed mainly by top pressure which is replacing manual bar pumps. One or two pubs still serve direct from the cask.

5   GEORGE BATEMAN & SONS LTD

'Good Honest Ales'

ADDRESS

Salem Bridge Brewery, Wainfleet, Skegness, Lincoln-shire. Tel Wainfleet 317/8.

RECOGNITION

Conspicuous red inn-signs with gold letters pointing the way to 'Good Honest Ales'. The name of the pub is also on the sign.

TIED HOUSES

There are 140 licensed houses in villages and market towns within a forty-mile radius of Wainfleet with a concentration around Wainfleet itself. The northern outpost is as far up the coast as Marsh Chapel (between Louth and Grimsby). You can drink 'Good Honest Ales' at Louth (Crosskeys, Thatch, Black Bull), Nettleham (just north-east of Lincoln), Horn-castle (three here easily found), south of here at Woodhall Spa, Coningsby and Ruskington (just north of Sleaford). Then further south at Holbeach, Fos-dyke, Surfleet and Risegate. There is also some free trade in this area.

BEERS

Draught   Bitter. Malty flavoured with above-aver-age hopping rate.
Light Mild. Not unlike the bitter in flavour but lower gravity.

Bottled   Light Dinner Ale. A low gravity light ale.
India Pale Ale. Medium gravity.
Nut Brown Ale. A lightish gravity brown
ale.
Double Brown. Medium gravity.

Draught beers are dispensed by manual bar pumps, direct from wooden casks, or in some cases by electric pumps.

6   DANIEL BATHAM & SON LTD

'Blessing of your heart;
you brew good ale'—Shakespeare

ADDRESS

The Delph Brewery, Brierley Hill, Staffs. Tel 77229.
Brierley Hill is in the rolling hills of the Black Country about twelve miles west of Birmingham.

RECOGNITION

'Batham's prize and diploma beer' is usually written on the pub's wall. Sometimes other slogans are to be seen such as 'Good health, good Delph'; or 'Batham's traditional home brewed mild and bitter ales'.

TIED HOUSES

Altogether there are 8 of these, two of which are at Brierley Hill itself (The Holly Bush, Pensnett, and the Vine in Delph Road next to the brewery). There are one each at Kinver (Plough & Harrow), Dudley (Lamp Tavern), and Stourbridge (Royal Exchange). Another three are further afield at Broadwater (Hare and Hounds, near Kidderminster), Shenstone (Plough, also near Kidderminster) and Chaddesley Corbet (Swan, between Kidderminster and Bromsgrove). There is also some free trade in the area.

BEERS

All beers brewed at the Delph Brewery are draught. There are a well balanced bitter with a good flavour and a light mild. There is also a strong dark mild. Bottled beers were once brewed at Delph but now bottled and keg beers are supplied by arrangement with Ind Coope, Guiness, Scottish & Newcastle and Whitbread. Manual bar pulls are used for dispensing the draught beers from wooden casks.

7   BEARD & CO (LEWES) LTD

'Draught Sussex Bitter'

Note   See also under 38 Harvey & Son (Lewes) Ltd, who brew for both Beard and Harvey.

ADDRESS

Star Lane Brewery, Fisher Street, Lewes, Sussex. Tel 4993.

Lewes is the county town of Sussex and is eight miles north-east of Brighton.

RECOGNITION

Usually 'Beard & Co' is written on the pub wall, or

'Beards'. Sometimes also 'Noted Ales, Wines and Spirits'. 'Draught Sussex Bitter sold here' is written on an orange plaque on an outside wall.

TIED HOUSES

There are 26 of these covering a wide area in East Sussex. There are 5 in Lewes itself and a Beard house can be found in the villages just north at Ringmer, East Chiltington, Isfield, Chailey, Newick and Scaynes Hill (Sloop Inn to the north of the village). Then a little further north towards Crawley at Horsted Keynes, Ardingly, Balcombe (outside on the Horley road), West Hoathly and Crawley Down. In the countryside to the north and north-east of Hailsham there are Beard houses at Lower Dicker, Vines Cross, Rushlake Green, Dallington, Mayfield (Brewers Arms) and Burwash; and further north at Tunbridge Wells (High Brooms Hotel). Then along the coast at Seaford (Wellington), Rottingdean (Black Horse) and just inland from Brighton at Patcham (Black Lion).

BEERS

Draught	Bitter. A nutty flavoured draught beer not usually in Beard houses but is in some Harvey houses.
	Best Bitter. Stronger and a little sweeter.
	Mild. A pleasant dry dark mild.
	XXXX (Old). A strong dark ale.
Keg	Keg Bitter. The Best Bitter in container.
Bottled	IPA. A pale ale.
	Blue Label. A stronger pale ale.
	Nut Brown. A medium sweet brown ale.

Exhibition Brown. Stronger than the
Nut Brown.
Sweet Stout.
Elizabethan Ale. Barley Wine.

A top pressure system and bar pumps are both used
to dispense draught beers.

8   BODDINGTONS' BREWERIES LTD

'Beer brewed in the finest tradition naturally'

ADDRESS

Strangeways Brewery, Manchester 3, Lancs. Tel
061-832-9891.

Manchester, capital of the cotton manufacturing
district of south-east Lancs, is the business, banking
and distribution centre for a number of surrounding
towns. It is a densely populated area and well known
for its friendly atmosphere.

Boddingtons' is Manchester's oldest brewery, dating back to 1778. It is very close to the city centre
and extensive bomb damage during the war triggered
off an extensive modernisation programme and
acquisition of modern equipment.

RECOGNITION

The house sign is a conspicuous yellow barrel on
which are two bees on a brown background and on
which is written 'Boddingtons' in white letters. Sometimes 'Boddingtons Beer' is displayed on the wall of
the pub.

TIED HOUSES

There are about 280 Boddington houses from Carnforth just north of Morecambe in North Lancs to Crewe in the south. They can be found in the counties of Lancashire, Cheshire, a little of Derbyshire (the Glossop area just east of Manchester), one house in Yorkshire (at Kinsley, south-east of Wakefield) and one in Staffs (at Rushton Spencer, which is near Leek). The main towns for Boddingtons' Ales are Manchester, Salford, Stockport, Macclesfield, Preston, Rochdale, Blackpool and the Fylde Coast. There is a free trade in the above areas.

BEERS

Draught	Bitter. A well hopped draught beer with a strong local following.
	Mild. Dark and medium sweet.
	Best Mild. A stronger mild.
Bottled	Boddington Light. A light dinner ale approaching a lager in its character.
	Strong Ale. A barley wine.
	Boddington Nut Brown. A sweet brown ale.
	Boddington Extra Stout. A sweet stout.

Draught beers are dispensed by manual bar pumps or by electric pumps.

9   BORDER BREWERIES (WREXHAM) LTD

'The Prince of Ales'

ADDRESS

Wrexham, Denbighshire, North Wales. Tel 3533.

For centuries Wrexham has been a brewing centre, and by the end of the last century there were 19 commercial breweries in the town. Two of these— F.W. Soames & Co and the Island Green Brewery Co Ltd—amalgamated with a third from Oswestry— Dorsett Owen & Co—to become Border Breweries (Wrexham) Ltd on 1 January 1932.

To supply their water for brewing, Border have two wells of their own, each about 130 feet deep.

Two brewery coopers repair the firm's wooden casks (many have now been replaced by metal ones) which are needed for their 'draught beer from the wood' trade.

RECOGNITION

Border houses vary from old traditional styles to modern designs but they all depict a red dragon rampant. Some houses have illuminated signs and there are also pictorial signs. The name 'Border' may be written on the wall of the pub. There are many variants—look out for the name 'Border' and a picture or outline of a red dragon.

TIED HOUSES

There are 170 tenanted and 20 managed houses serving the three main centres of Wrexham, Oswestry and Shrewsbury and many surrounding towns and villages. However, the trading area is much greater than the Anglo-Welsh frontiers, and the 200 or so pubs extend well into England as far as the Potteries and in the opposite direction as far as the north and west coasts of Wales. To the north, Border houses may be found in the Mold and Chester areas and to the south as far as Newtown in Montgomeryshire.

There is a free trade, and Border own 10 wine and spirit outlets.

BEERS

A range of draught beers which includes a draught bitter with quite a hoppy flavour, a light mild which is more like a bitter, and a medium and stronger dark mild. Draught beers may be supplied in tank form after conditioning at the brewery and dispensing systems include top pressure and manual bar pumps. There is a keg bitter called Dragon Keg.

Bottled beers include a pale ale, Exhibition (a stronger pale ale), Royal Wrexham Ale (a barley wine), a brown ale and a strong brown ale.

10   S.A. BRAIN & CO LTD

'Its Brains you want'

ADDRESS

The Old Brewery, St Mary Street, Cardiff, South Wales. Tel 25441/4.

The brewery is right in the centre of Cardiff not far from the castle.

RECOGNITION

Brains houses are easily spotted by the name 'Brains' being written on the wall of the pub in various colours, but most often in blue. 'Brains Red Dragon Beer' is also a slogan which may be seen.

TIED HOUSES

Over 100 of these in the Cardiff area and westwards as far as Swansea (Adam & Eve; Vivian Arms) and in many of the towns and villages in between. Penarth and Barry near Cardiff have Brain pubs, so do Porthcawl and nearby Newton which are further west along the coast. On the road to Swansea the 'Brains' sign can be seen at Bonvilston and Cowbridge. There is some free trade within these areas.

BEERS

Draught	Draught Bitter. A well balanced draught beer.
	SA Best Draught Bitter. Stronger than the above.
	Red Dragon Draught Dark. A well flavoured dark beer.
Keg	Tudor Light.
	Gold Dragon. A stronger keg bitter.
Bottled	Pale Ale.
	IPA. Stronger than the pale ale.
	Amber Ale. The strongest pale ale.
	Extra Stout. Medium sweet.
	Strong Ale.

Draught beers are dispensed mostly by manual bar pumps and occasionally by a top pressure system.

11   W.H. BRAKSPEAR & SONS LTD

'Henley Brewery'

ADDRESS

The Brewery, Henley-on-Thames, Oxfordshire. Tel 3636/7.

Henley, a riverside town famous for its rowing regatta, lies on the north bank of the Thames, 36 miles due west of London and 8 miles north-east of Reading.

RECOGNITION

Tied houses are distinguished by 'Henley Brewery' being written on the pub's wall or sign, which is predominantly dark blue.

TIED HOUSES

There are about 130 picturesque and friendly 'Henley Brewery' pubs in Henley and many surrounding towns and villages. They are easily found on and within an imaginary circle starting at High Wycombe (Wendover Arms in Desborough Avenue), then going clockwise through Marlow (Chequers in High St and Clayton Arms in Oxford Road), Maidenhead (Hand and Flowers in Queen St; Vine, Market St), Holyport, Wokingham (Crooked Billet, Dukes Head, Hope & Anchor, Red Lion), Reading (Dove, Orts Rd; Rising Sun, Forbury Rd; Old House at Home, Warren Row; Sun, Whitchurch Hill; Meadway at Tilehurst; at Sonning Common; Gallowstree Common; and others easily found in Caversham), Goring-on-Thames, Blewbury, Wallingford (Cross Keys; Coachmakers Arms; Kings Head), Benson, Warborough, Berrick Salome, South Weston, Kingston Blount and back to High

Wycombe. Outside this circle look for the blue sign at Sandhurst near Camberley (Wellington Arms), Finch-ampstead (Queen's Oak) and Mortimer West End to the south-west of Reading (Turners Arms).

BEERS

Draught	Pale Ale. A well hopped draught bitter with above-average flavour.
	SBA—Special Bitter Ale. A stronger bitter.
	XXX Mild. A dark beer.
	XXXX. A stronger dark beer ('Old'—available in a very few pubs all the year round).
Keg	Beehive Keg. Distinctively flavoured for a keg beer. Chilled and filtered but not pasteurised.
Bottled	Light Ale.
	Pale Ale.
	Henley Strong Ale.
	These three pale ales are in ascending order of strength.
	Brown Ale.
	Henley Lager.

Draught beers are drawn direct from the cask (usually wooden) or via beer engine manual bar pumps.

12   MATTHEW BROWN & CO LTD

'Lion Ales'

ADDRESS

Lion Brewery, Blackburn, Lancs. Tel 52471.
 Blackburn, an industrial town with a modern,

covered shopping centre and overhead car park, is 24 miles north of Manchester and 8 miles east of the M6 motorway.

RECOGNITION

Easy to recognise by the large Red Lion sign on the wall pointing the way to 'Lion Ales'. The name of the pub is in separate individual letters, and there is an extensive redevelopment and improvement programme which is linked to the common theme of the Red Lion.

TIED HOUSES

Over 600 of these which are well distributed over a large area in Lancashire and Cumberland as follows.

In Lancashire. Radiating out from Blackburn and in a clockwise direction in the towns of Colne, Accrington, Darwen, Astley Bridge near Bolton, Ashton-in-Makerfield, Wigan, Chorley, Leyland, Southport, Preston, Blackpool, Coniston and Dalton-in-Furness, and many villages in between.

In Cumberland. At Cleator Moor, Whitehaven, Workington, Maryport, Cockermouth and Keswick.

There are many free trade outlets in these areas and also in Westmorland.

BEERS

Draught	Bitter. A well balanced draught beer.
	Mild. A darkish mild.
Keg	Keg Bitter.
	Lion Lager.

Bottled   Light Ale.
              Crystal. A slightly stronger light ale.
              Export IPA. A strong light ale.
              Kings Ale. A barley wine.
              Brown Ale. The mild in bottle.
              Lion Stout. Medium sweet.
              Lion Lager.

Draught beers are dispensed by manual bar pumps which are being replaced by a top pressure system and container beers.

13   BUCKLEY'S BREWERY LTD

'The friendly draught'

ADDRESS

The Brewery, Llanelli, Carmarthenshire, South Wales. Tel 58441.

Llanelli, a town famous for its rugby club and tin plate, lies just west of Swansea and overlooks Carmarthen Bay. The nearby county town of Carmarthen enjoys all day opening on Mondays, Wednesdays, Thursdays and Saturdays; and the first Friday in the month. These are market days for the predominantly farming area.

RECOGNITION

A distinctive white sign with the figure of a Bard drinking from a horn, and 'Buckley's Welsh Ales' in various colours but usually blue or mauve. 'Buckley's Beers' is sometimes written on the pub wall. The name of the pub is written along the bottom of the sign.

TIED HOUSES

Approximately 180 of these in Llanelli and radiating out from there at Burry Port, Kidwelly, Carmarthen, Llandilo, Ammanford, and Pontardulais. Then west of Carmarthen at St Clears, Whitland and Pembroke, and along the north-west coast to Cardigan and New Quay. Further inland Buckley's beers can be found at Tregaron. East of Llanelli look out for the drinking Bard at Swansea (eg Rhymbuck on the road out to the west and partly owned, Travellers Well at Cwmbwlla, Coopers Arms on the road out to the east) and Neath (the Bard), just north at Gorseinon and Pontardawe and at Llandovery which is not far west of Brecon. There is a new pub at Porthcawl (Seagull). Also many villages between these towns.

There is a flourishing free trade.

BEERS

Draught	SB—Standard Bitter.
	BB—Best Bitter. A little stronger.
	Both of these are very well hopped beers with a good flavour. The BB is in all houses and the SB only in some (an example in the Llanelli area is the Cornish Inn at Burry Port).
	Bulk Beer. This is the BB filtered for bulk delivery (container beer) to the trade.
	Mild. A medium dark, hoppy flavoured beer.
Keg	Welcome Keg. The equivalent of the BB in keg.
Bottled	Bitter Ale. Equivalent to the SB in bottle.

Welsh Ale. A stronger light ale.

Brown Ale. Medium sweet.

PBA. A sweet mild ale.

Draught beers are dispensed by electric pumps (some casks have a light covering of CO_2), top pressure, manual bar pumps, or direct from the cask.

14   BURT & CO

'Ventnor Ales'

'Island Brewery'

ADDRESS

High Street, Ventnor, Isle of Wight. Tel 153.

Ventnor is a seaside resort on the south-east coast of the island situated on a series of terraces below the steep face of St Boniface Down. The brewery is sited beneath the slopes of this down because there is an abundant supply of suitable spring water. Burt of Ventnor is one of the smallest breweries in the country, and owned today by the Philips family who often deliver the beer themselves if staff is short. It is still very much a family concern. The brewery was put out of action by bombs during the war, since when a completely new brewhouse has been built.

RECOGNITION

'Burt & Co' may be written on the pub wall, or 'Burt's Ventnor Ales', or it may be 'Burt's Ales Ventnor Brewery'. Whatever it is, the name Burt or Ventnor can be seen in most cases.

TIED HOUSES

There are 11 of these, mostly in the south-east of the island. In Ventnor itself there are 6—Central Hotel which is residential; behind here the Hole in the Wall (which used to be the Central Tap); Terminus Hotel at the foot of the down and near the old railway station; Mill Bay Hotel opposite the pier; Volunteer Inn near the bus station; and Walmer Castle Inn near the brewery. At Wroxall, a village behind Ventnor, there is the Star Hotel. At Shanklin there is the Chine Inn close to the sea, reputed to have smuggling connections. And between there and Sandown there is the Stag Inn at Lake. At the other end of the island Burt's Ales may be drunk at Freshwater at the residential Royal Standard Hotel, and near the middle on the Arreton Downs there is the Hare and Hounds inn and roadhouse.

There is a flourishing free trade in hotels, holiday camps and clubs. A booklet on the 'Island Brewery' has been published and can be obtained from the brewery or one of the pubs.

BEERS

Draught   Bitter—LB. A well-hopped brew but not in every pub.

Special Bitter—VPA. The 'Best Bitter' and slightly stronger.

Mild—BMA. A dark mild with an agreeable dryish flavour. A special blend of British and continental hops is used which gives the beer a pleasant, distinctive flavour.

Bottled   Ventnor Pale Ale.
              Golden IPA. A strongish pale ale.
              Nut Brown Ale. Medium sweet.
              Burt's Strong Brown. Stronger and
              sweeter.

Draught beers are dispensed by top pressure or in some cases by manual bar pumps (Volunteer, Mill Bay).

15   BURTONWOOD BREWERY CO (FORSHAWS) LTD

'Big taste beers'

ADDRESS

Bold Lane, Burtonwood, Warrington, Lancs. Tel Newton-le-Willows 4281.

Burtonwood is to the north-west of Warrington and about halfway between Manchester and Liverpool.

The water for brewing comes from a number of deep wells which are situated around the brewery.

RECOGNITION

'Burtonwood Ales' is usually written on the wall of the pub or it may be written on a conspicuous yellow board. There may also be a maroon hanging sign.

TIED HOUSES

There are over 300 licensed houses covering a wide area in the north-west and North Wales as follows.

In Lancashire. Nearly 150 pubs mainly concentrated within a wide area from Preston down the coast to the Mersey, across to Manchester and north to Blacko above Nelson. Outside this area there is a house at Blackpool, one at Barkisland (near Elland, Yorks) and one in Yorkshire at Jack Bridge near Hebden Bridge.

In Cheshire and Staffordshire. Over 50 spread over a wide area with the biggest concentration east and south of Stoke-on-Trent, then west to Whitchurch and up to Chester and Birkenhead.

In North Wales. Over 100 covering the whole of North Wales, and in Mid Wales down to Dolgellau on the coast and inland as far south as Newtown, Montgomery and district.

There are another 15 pubs in Anglesey extending all over the island.

A large number of Burtonwood houses offer food and accommodation and a booklet describing all the houses can be obtained at the brewery.

There is a free trade within the above areas.

BEERS

Draught	Bitter. A well-balanced draught beer.
	Mild. A dark mild.
Bottled	LXR Pale Ale. A normal pale ale.
	Special Pale Ale. Stronger than the above.
	Top Hat. A strong ale.
	Export. A strong lager-type pale ale.
	Buckle Dark Ale. A strong dark beer.
	Super Brown Ale. Medium sweet.
	Burtonwood Stout. A medium sweet stout.

Draught beers are dispensed by means of an electric metering system and also by manual bar pumps.

16   J.W. CAMERON & CO LTD

'The mightiest of beers'

ADDRESS

Greenbank Offices, Lion Brewery, Hartlepool, Co Durham. Tel 66666.

Hartlepool is an industrial town on the north-east coast and a few miles to the north of Teesside.

RECOGNITION

Signs include a yellow (sometimes white) barrel-shaped or square illuminated sign hanging outside the pub. A red lion rampant is on the sign, across which is written 'Camerons' on a white background. Sometimes there is a pictorial sign with 'Camerons' written on a red strip below the sign. The name of the pub is usually in red letters on a pale yellow background.

TIED HOUSES

Around 700 or more well spread out in the counties of Durham and Yorkshire (especially to the east of the county) and easily found over a large part of north-east England.

BEERS

These include a well-balanced Best Bitter, a dark

mild, and Strongarm Ale—a well-flavoured strong bitter which is not at all sweet and mostly found in the Hartlepool and Teesside districts (but also in other areas). Keg beers such as Target Keg and Icegold Lager; and among the bottled beers are Special Light Ale, Export Ale, Strongarm, Old Stranton Barley Wine, and Special Brown Ale.

Draught beers are dispensed in most cases by a metering system with electric pumps or by manual bar pumps.

17   CARLISLE AND DISTRICT STATE MANAGEMENT SCHEME

ADDRESS

19, Castle Street, Carlisle, Cumberland. Tel 25213; and Old Brewery, Caldewgate, Carlisle.

Carlisle is the county town of Cumberland and was an important border fortress, but to the beer drinker Carlisle is the place where for the last fifty years or so the beer has been provided by the state—although not for much longer, because the government announced plans to discontinue the scheme soon after attaining power in 1970.

It all started during World War I when the biggest munitions factory in the Empire had been built in the Scottish village of Gretna—perhaps better known for its romantic associations with elopements. Gretna is only nine miles from Carlisle, and thousands of Irish workers had descended on the district to build and man the factory. Heavy drinking became the order of the day—and night—and by early 1916 'disorder had spread to such an extent as to threaten to undermine the ordinary social life of the city', according to an official report.

Whether this was the real reason, whether the war-effort was being undermined, or whether it was just opportune for Lloyd George, the Minister of Munitions, with his puritanical background, is speculation. Whatever the reason, it was decided in the middle of 1916 that the whole of the drink trade in the city and outlying districts should be placed under the control of the Liquor Control Board. So the 'experiment'—which it was always called by official-dom—began, and was to continue for more than half a century. Before the takeover of brewing in Carlisle there were four breweries, but only one was retained—the Carlisle Old Brewery in Caldewgate—where all production was centralised. Apart from Carlisle and Gretna, where the pubs, hotels and off-licences were acquired by the board, there was also the Cromarty Firth Scheme (near a submarine base), but this obtained all its beer from private Scottish brewers.

So for the rest of the war drinking was very tightly controlled by the government; but when the war was over it was assumed by one and all that the experiment would end and private industry would once again satisfy the thirsts of the local residents, now that the munitions workers had gone home.

But this was not to be. Although the Control Board disappeared, it popped up again in the guise of the Carlisle and District State Management Scheme, which, however, did adopt a much broader outlook. Not only that, it has often been said that the scheme bent over backwards to satisfy customers, and as the years went by it became an accepted part of the local scene, and good quality beer has always been sold at reasonable prices.

One of the main criticisms voiced was that the scheme had created too rigid a monopoly—which is ironic, in view of the monopolies created by some private brewers that have developed all over the country without hindrance from the government. It is also unjustified, because the average Carlisle Brewery house offered a far greater choice of beers than many pubs owned by private brewers.

Some of the smaller and less profitable pubs have been offered on sale to sitting landlords where the trade was four equivalent barrels or less (a barrel is 36 gallons and by 'equivalent' is meant casks and bottles etc converted to barrels). The more profitable pubs have not been so offered. This seems to be unfair on the landlord who has managed to build up a good trade.

So after half a century of excellent service to Carlisle and District, the State Management Scheme is being wound up. After World War I, when it was no longer needed, it was continued; now when it has become accepted it is to be ended—apparently against the wishes of the local people. Not a very good example of democracy at work.

RECOGNITION AND TIED HOUSES

Carlisle beer was not sold by advertising, and apart from the name of the pub there was no indication as to the brewery. There were nearly 170 tied or managed houses owned by the scheme, mostly in Carlisle but also in outlying districts within a radius of 10-30 miles.

BEERS

Draught beers were a well-flavoured draught bitter with a good hop rate and a dark mild. Both were sold in casks or tanks or as keg beer. Bottled beers were Light Ale, Nut Brown Ale and Export (a strong light ale). In addition there were usually over twenty brands of beer from other brewers in Carlisle pubs—draught, keg and bottled. Draught beers were dispensed by manual bar pumps, electric pumps with meters or top pressure CO_2.

18   CASTLETOWN BREWERY LTD

'Ale of Man'

ADDRESS

Victoria Road, Castletown, Isle of Man. Tel 2561/2/3.

The brewery lies opposite Rushen Catle.

In the Isle of Man the price of beer is slightly lower than on the mainland of Britain because of the smaller beer duty imposed by the Manx government. All beers brewed in the Isle of Man are subject to an old Manx 'Pure Beer Act' in force since 1874 which says that 'no ingredients other than malt, hops and sugar are used in brewing. A brewer is liable to a penalty of £300 and the confiscation of his entire plant and stock if this Act is contravened . . .'

RECOGNITION

'Castletown Ales' may be written on the pub wall,

but in many cases there is no distinguishing name at all. However, Castletown Brewery pubs can usually be easily recognised, being in the house colours of black and white—a white building with black woodwork.

TIED HOUSES

There are nearly 40 of these and they are evenly spread out all over the island with a fair sprinkling up north along the TT coast. A number of the houses are residential.

BEERS

Draught	Bitter. A well-balanced draught beer.
	Mild. A medium light mild.
Bottled	Castletown Pale Ale.
	Castletown Nut Brown. A medium sweet brown ale.
	Castletown Liqueur Barley Wine. A barley wine.

Jubilee Stout (of Bass Charrington) is brewed here and Carling's Lager is in all houses in draught (keg) or bottle.

Draught beers are dispensed by manual bar pumps or from the cask.

19   G.E. COOK & SONS LTD

ADDRESS

Tidings Hill Brewery, Halstead, Essex. Tel 2089.

Halstead is a small country town in north-east Essex not far from the Suffolk border.

G.E. Cook & Sons Ltd operate entirely within the free trade and as a supplier for the home. There is a chain of retail branches in north and east Essex—at Braintree, Chelmsford, Colchester, Dovercourt, Halstead and Writtle; and in Suffolk at Ipswich. Also a fleet of vans doing door-to-door delivery.

Cook & Sons import their own sherry and also a range of wines. Most of the beer production is for bottling but one beer is sold in draught form and supplied to private customers at a few days' notice in pins (4½ gallons).

BEERS

Draught   Cook's Best Bitter. A lightly hopped draught bitter which is only supplied to private customers, in aluminium casks (pins).

Bottled   Golden Ale. A pale ale.
Country Brew. A well-flavoured strong pale ale with a good local following.
Nut Brown Ale. A medium sweet brown ale.
Oatmeal Stout. A dryish stout.

20   W.M. DARLEY LTD

'Symbol of good ale'

ADDRESS

The Brewery, Thorne, Doncaster, Yorkshire. Tel Thorne 81233.

Thorne is a small town about ten miles east of

Doncaster. It has a church of around AD 1300 and lies on the western edge of a great peat moor.

RECOGNITION

The 'symbol of good ale' is a mailed charger's head to be seen outside all Darley houses on an illuminated sign on which is also written 'Darley's Ales'. The sign is beehive-shaped. There may be a board with the grey charger on a green background and 'Darley's Ales' written in gold letters on a green background.

TIED HOUSES

There are over 100 of these and they can be found in Thorne itself and its surroundings (eg Carlton on the Selby road); in Castleford, Normanton, Pontefract and Doncaster to the west; to the north-east in Hull, Beverley and Bridlington; in Lincolnshire at Clee-thorpes and Scunthorpe. There is also a free trade.

BEERS

Draught	Darley's IPA. A pleasantly flavoured well-balanced bitter.
	Darley's Dark. A dark mild.
Keg	Darley's Keg. Keg bitter.
Bottled	East India Pale Ale.
	Amber Ale. A lighter pale ale.
	Special Mild Ale. Equivalent to the draught mild.
	Nut Brown Ale.
	Barley Cream. A medium sweet stout.

Draught beers are dispensed by manual bar pumps or electric pumps.

21 DAVENPORTS C.B. & BREWERY (HOLDINGS) LTD

'Beer at home'

ADDRESS

The Brewery, Bath Row, Birmingham, Warwickshire. Tel 021-643-5021.

Birmingham, Britain's foremost metal-working town and centre of an important industrial area, is Britain's second largest city and has a new, modern centre.

RECOGNITION

Look for the name 'Davenports' written on the wall, usually in red. Sometimes there is a shield by the front door with a malt and hops symbol.

TIED HOUSES

There are just over 100 of these spread over a very wide area. This is practicable because Davenports are famous for their 'beer at home' trade (a home delivery service) and their free trade in many clubs in the country. So they have a number of strategically placed distribution depots. Tied houses can be found in the following areas.

In the Birmingham area. Spread over Greater Birmingham as follows. In Birmingham central (Australian Bar, Lee Tavern, White Lion); Northfield (Bell, Black Horse); Solihull (Boat); Bentley Heath

(Drum & Monkey); Halesowen (Hare & Hounds, Queens Head); Kings Norton (Navigation Inn); Earlswood (Reservoir Hotel); Portway (Rose & Crown); Stuckley (Three Horseshoes); Meer End (Tipperary); Rowley Regis (Vine); Sutton Coldfield (White Horse); Bartley Green (Woodcock).

In Coventry, Leamington, Rugby and Warwick areas. At Warwick (Punch Bowl, Red Lion, Woodman, Zetland); Leamington (Hope Tavern, Coach & Horses); and nearby at Radford Semele and Whitnash; further south-east at Ufton, Ladbroke, Napton, Priors Marston, Southam and Long Itchington; at Kenilworth (Virgins & Castle); Stratford (Old Tramway); east of Coventry and north of Rugby at Newbold-on-Avon and north-west of Coventry at Fillongley. Also at Bascote Heath and Canley.

In the East Midlands. Well scattered and at Shardlow near Derby; Osgathorpe west of Loughborough; Skeffington between Leicester and Uppingham; Northampton (Saddlers Arms) and Grendon to the east; and in between at Market Harborough (Harborough Lounge) and Bitteswell further west.

In Oxfordshire. Just one (Saye & Sele) at Broughton near Banbury.

In Shropshire. Just two houses—at Craven Arms and Hopton Wafers.

In Staffordshire. Three—at Lichfield (Duke of York); and at Kinver and Wordsley, both near Stourbridge.

In Worcestershire. In Worcester (Bedwardine, Coventry Arms, Vine); south-west at Bransford on the Hereford road; south at Upton-upon-Severn (Talbot Head), Defford and Beckford on the Evesham—Cheltenham road; well to the west at Stoke Prior; north of Worcester at Fernhill Heath; at

Droitwich (Castle, Star & Garter); Upton Warren; near Bronsgrove (Dodford Inn, Park Gate Inn); Catshill; Redditch (Foxlydiate Hotel); Bewdley (Running Horse, Talbot); Kidderminster (Station Inn); and at Wollaston, Iverley and Old Swinford.

A map giving all the houses in the above areas is usually displayed in a bar or corridor of the pub.

In addition to the above, outposts are at Bristol (Bay Horse), Wallasey (Nelson), Leeds (Seacroft), Nottingham (Mechanics Arms, Cricketers Rest), Corby (Phoenix), and Usk in South Wales (The Bridge). There are also several in the Abergavenny area of South Wales and west of here at Crickhowel.

BEERS

Draught	Bitter. Well hopped and pleasantly flavoured.
	Mild. A dark mild.
Keg	Drum Bitter.
	Drum Mild.
	These are also available in 4 and 7 pint cans with a special sparklet tap so the can does not have to be drunk all at once.
	Continental Lager.
Bottled	Pale Ale.
	Best Bitter. More bitter than the pale ale and a little weaker.
	Top Brew. A very strong and well-flavoured dark ale.
	Brown Ale.
	Continental Lager.

Draught beers are dispensed by manual bar pulls, top

pressure or electric pumps. Draught beers have round, gold bar mountings whereas keg beer bar mountings are shaped like drums; so the two are easily distinguishable to the customer.

22   J.A. DEVENISH & CO LTD.

'The Beers of the South West'

ADDRESS

Trinity House, 15 Trinity St, Weymouth, Dorset. Tel 3922.
    Devenish brew at the seaside resort of Weymouth and also at Redruth (Tel 5304), Cornwall.

RECOGNITION

Conspicuous bright green signboards with the pub's name in gold and 'Devenish' written in old English script. The house sign is a demi-tiger (a heraldic term) holding a crosslet (devised from the Devenish family crest and nicknamed 'Herbert the Tiger'). 'The best beers in the South West' is a common motto used on bar towels and other utensils.

TIED HOUSES

Devenish houses can be found over a very wide area, with the biggest concentrations in Dorset, radiating out from Weymouth, and in the Redruth district of

Cornwall. Starting in the extreme south-west, look for the green signs as follows.

In Cornwall. Most of the 185 licensed houses are in the western half but also extend as far as Launceston, nearby Tregadillet and Liskeard, with a sprinkling in the areas of Wadebridge, Bodmin and Lostwithiel.

In Devon. Here the 53 houses are mainly east of Exeter and along and south of the A30 as far as Honiton and along the coast. There is a sprinkling just to the north at Pinhoe, Silverton, Whimple and Talaton. In Exeter there are several, including a brand new one, and others are to the south at Teignmouth, to the west at Ide, Cheriton Bishop and Crediton, then further north at Bickington and Barnstaple.

In Dorset. There are 98 with 56 in Weymouth itself. Then extending north to Cerne Abbas, west to Lyme Regis, east to Wimborne and between Poole and the coast. The thatch-roofed Smiths Arms at Godmanstone north of Dorchester is one of the smallest in England.

In Gloucestershire. At Bristol in Stokes Croft.

In Hampshire. At Bournemouth, Lymington and Mudeford.

In Somerset. At Bath, Crewkerne and East Coker, which is south-west of Yeovil.

In Wiltshire. At Marlborough, Salisbury and Swindon.

In all there are over 400 licensed houses with an extensive free trade in the area. Brochures can be obtained from both breweries listing and mapping the pubs.

BEERS

Draught   Bitter. A pleasant, well hopped beer.

	Wessex IPA. As above but stronger.
	XXX Mild. A dark mild.
Keg	Saxon Bitter. A keg bitter which is also in 5-pint take-home sealed cans.
	Dark Keg. A sweet mild in container.
	Whitbread Tankard is brewed and available in the pubs. It has replaced Devenish Highlife Keg Bitter.
Bottled	Light Ale.
	Wessex Pale Ale. Considerably stronger.
	Crabber's Nip. A barley wine.
	Bosun Brown Ale. A sweet brown ale.
	S-W Stout. Medium sweet.

A new lager—Viking Lager—was recently introduced and will be available in bottle and on draught.

Draught beers may be dispensed by top pressure (in the majority), via bar pumps or direct from a metal cask. A large proportion of the houses serve one or more cooled beers.

23   DUDGEON & CO LTD

'Proved by test, Scotland's best'
'Here's the brew for you'

ADDRESS
Belhaven Brewery, Dunbar, East Lothian, Scotland. Tel 2134.

Dunbar is an ancient sea port and summer resort close to a famous golfing coastline.

Belhaven is Scotland's oldest independent brewery and has been brewing since 1719. It has an outstanding record, for its size, in brewer's exhibitions. When

Boswell, Samuel Johnson's biographer, stopped at Dunbar, he said 'the best small beer I ever had'. The Emperor of Austria was also familiar with Belhaven ales and said 'Belhaven beer is the Burgundy of Scotland . . . Bavaria cannot produce the like'.

Belhaven advises on the brewing of, and bottles, the Traquair House Ale brewed at Traquair House, Innerleithen (see p 78).

RECOGNITION

There is a black and white plaque on which is written 'Belhaven prize winning ales and stout' on the wall of the pubs. Also written on the wall may be 'Belhaven Prize Ales'.

TIED HOUSES

There are 7 of these, 2 of which are at Belhaven (just outside Dunbar on the Edinburgh road) and at West Barns next door. There is one at East Linton which lies just off the main road (A1) to Edinburgh, and the remaining 4 are all at Dunbar.

There is a very flourishing free trade, and clubs, hotels, free pubs in East Lothian and across to Glasgow are, in many cases, supplied with Belhaven beers.

BEERS
Draught   Export.
               Heavy (or Special).

Light B.

These are draught bitters in descending order of strength, supplied either in casks or tanks. The Export is sold mainly in the free trade.

Bottled   Belhaven Pale Ale.

Export Prize Ale.

Strong Ale.

These three are pale ales in ascending order of strength.

No 1 Stout. A medium sweet stout.

Dunbar Sweet Stout.

Trinidad Stout. This is a dryish stout also exported to Anguilla, Jamaica, St Kitts, Tahiti, and Trinidad.

Draught beers are mostly dispensed by top pressure.

24   ELDRIDGE, POPE & CO LTD

'Huntsman Ales the beer of Wessex'

ADDRESS

Dorchester Brewery, Dorchester, Dorset. Tel 4801.

Dorchester has been a brewing town for over 300 years, and Eldridge, Pope have been brewing beer since 1837. The company is also a wine importer and has a chain of retail shops throughout Dorset, Hampshire and Somerset.

RECOGNITION

An illuminated sign with a picture of a jovial huntsman raising a glass of beer above the name

'Huntsman'. 'Huntsman Ales' is usually written in red or white letters on the wall of the pub, and some pubs have pictorial signs.

TIED HOUSES

There are around 200 Huntsman pubs covering the county of Dorset and extending into Hampshire and Somerset. Going in a clockwise direction from Weymouth on the coast, they can be found as follows.

In the Weymouth area. 14 in Weymouth, in Portland and just north in the villages of Radipole and Upwey.

In the Dorchester area. 19 in the town and to the north at Cerne Abbas and Piddletrenthide.

In the Yeovil area. 5 in Yeovil and also to the west at Stoke-under-Ham, East Chinnock and Crewkerne.

In the Sherborne area. 5 in Sherborne, in Marston Magna to the north, Charlton Horethorne, North Cadbury, Lydford-on-Fosse and Doulting; to the east at Milborne Port, Stalbridge, Stalbridge Weston, and towards Blandford at Shillingstone; and to the south at Long Burton, Bradford Abbas and Yetminster.

In and around Shaftesbury. In Shaftesbury itself and to the north at Ansty and Tisbury.

Salisbury and surroundings. 8 in Salisbury and to the west at Fovant, Sutton Mandeville and Swallowcliffe; and southwards at Downton, Fordingbridge and Stuckton.

Winchester and surroundings. 12 in Winchester and south of here at Twyford, Eastleigh and Allbrook.

Portsmouth area. 7 here and at Southsea and to the north at North Boarhunt.

Southampton. 9 here and at nearby Redbridge.

In the New Forest. At Ringwood, Moortown, Poulner, Lymington, Pennington, Brockenhurst, Boldre and New Milton.

In the Bournemouth area. 20 in Bournemouth and at Christchurch and Bransgore.

In the Wimborne area. 3 in Wimborne.

In and around Poole. 11 in Poole and also at Parkstone, Broadstone and Hamworthy.

Many of the houses are residential, and a brochure with all important details can be obtained from the brewery. A map showing every town that has a Huntsman house is on a drip mat in the pubs.

There is an extensive free trade which stretches from Seaton in Devon to Taunton in Somerset and to towns on the Bristol Channel, then to Swindon and on a wide arc over the top of Salisbury and down to Winchester.

BEERS

Draught	Best Bitter. (Called Club Bitter in the free trade).
	Special IPA.
	These are draught bitters with a full, malty flavour. The IPA is the strongest.
	XXXX. A strong, dark old ale which is in pubs where requested by the landlord, and is available over a 'long' winter period.
	Double Mild. A dark mild.
Keg	Crystal Bright. A keg bitter.
	Master Keg. A higher-gravity keg bitter.
	Konig Lager.
Bottled	Crystal Light Ale.

Page 133 (*above*) A horse-drawn dray of bygone years; (*below*) steam wagons such as this (1912) were used for deliveries at one time

Page 134 (*above*) Deliveries to a 'Huntsman' pub in Bournemouth, 1923; (*below*) a country delivery today by horse-drawn drays (from Southwold, Suffolk)

Green Top Pale Ale. Stronger, and the equivalent of the IPA.

Old Master Strong Ale. A strong pale ale.

Goldie Pale Barley Wine.

Dorset Brown Ale. Medium sweet.

Konig lager.

Konig Diabetic. A 'sugar-free' lager approved by the British Diabetic Association.

Konig Imperial de Luxe. A high gravity lager.

Hardy Ale. This is stated to be one of the strongest beers in the world and should last twenty-five years or more. It is brewed specially for Hardy Festivals and is in pint bottles and nips.

Cans   Homecan 7. A special bitter in a 7-pint can.

Draught beers are dispensed by top pressure and in a few cases direct from the cask.

25   ELGOOD & SONS LTD

'Elgood's Ales'

ADDRESS

North Brink Brewery, Wisbech, Cambs. Tel 3160.

Wisbech is a fenland town south of the Wash and fourteen miles south-west of Kings Lynn.

RECOGNITION

'Elgood's Ales' is generally written on the pub wall.

Pictorial signs, apart from two or three, are all hand-painted. The house sign is a greyhound with a key in its mouth—on labels and letter headings etc.

TIED HOUSES

There are 60-70 of these radiating out from Wisbech and extending as far as Peterborough—where there are three—and Whittlesey further south-west, then north at Spalding and Holbeach and into Norfolk at Kings Lynn. There is an Elgood house just inland from Hunstanton at Stanhoe; others south of Wisbech at March, Welney and Doddington, and in many of the villages between these towns.

BEERS

Draught	Bitter. A full-flavoured beer, lightly hopped.
	Mild. A slightly sweet dark mild.
Keg	Keg Bitter. Well-balanced and darker in colour than many keg beers.
Bottled	Pale Ale.
	Fenman. A strong pale ale.
	Brown Ale. Not too sweet.
	Russett Ale. A full sweet brown ale.
	Old English. A heavier, sweet beer most suited to winter drinking.
	Stout. Sweet.
	Iceberg Lager. With a pleasant flavour.

Draught beers are dispensed by bar pumps, top pressure or electric pumps.

26   EVERARDS BREWERY LTD

'Gentlemen, the Best'

ADDRESS

Tiger Brewery, 39 Castle Street, Leicester. Tel 56951.

The brewery itself is at Burton-on-Trent, but Leicester is the distribution centre.

RECOGNITION

Tied houses have an illuminated sign with a figure of a drinking man within a yellow circle, 'Everards' in red above, and the pub's name below. Signs are gradually changing over to outlined motifs descriptively portraying the name of the pub.

TIED HOUSES

There are nearly 130 licensed houses, 40 of which are in Leicester itself. Country houses are mostly within seven miles and all within thirty miles of Leicester. Outposts are at Repton just north-east of Burton-on-Trent, then in a clockwise direction at Loughborough, Hoby (between Loughborough and Melton Mowbray), Twyford to the south-east, Corby (Cottingham road), Kettering, Desborough (east of Market Harborough), Lutterworth and Stoke Golding near Hinckley, and in many villages within this area.

There is a free trade in the same area.

John Sarson & Son Ltd, wine merchants, are within the Everards organisation.

BEERS

Draught   Beacon Bitter. A well-balanced bitter

that is also supplied in canister form
conditioned and ready for consumption.
Tiger Draught. A stronger bitter.
Burton Mild. A dark mild.

Keg   Tiger Special Keg. A keg bitter.

Bottled   Amber Lite. A light ale.
Red Crown Bitter. A bottled 'Burton
Bitter', very well flavoured.
Tiger Special Ale. A stronger pale ale.
Gold Medal Barley Wine.
Nut Brown. Brown ale in pint bottles.
Bradgate Brown. Brown ale in small
bottles.
Meadowsweet Stout.

For draught beers a new system of dispensing has
been introduced—so far, into a few pubs. This is with
a covering of CO_2 exerting a very slight pressure, and
the motive power is supplied by compressed air which
does not come into contact with the beer. Top
pressure, electric pumps and manual bar pumps are
also used according to the pub's requirements.

27   THE FELINFOEL BREWERY CO LTD

'Felinfoel Ales best in Wales'

ADDRESS

Felinfoel Brewery, Llanelli, Carmarthenshire, South
Wales. Tel 3356/7.

Llanelli, famous for its rugby club and tinplate,
overlooks Carmarthen Bay just to the west of
Swansea.

The brewery is at Felinfoel which is a small town

adjoining Llanelli. Felinfoel was the first brewery in Britain to pioneer and introduce canned beers—as far back as December 1935.

RECOGNITION

Felinfoel houses are easily recognised by conspicuous green signboards depicting the Welsh red dragon. 'Felinfoel Ales', usually in cream letters, is written across the sign.

TIED HOUSES

There are 75-80 of these concentrated in the Llanelli area, and also widely distributed over Cardigan, Carmarthen and Pembroke. Just east of Llanelli there are Felinfoel houses at Gorseinon, Morriston and Pontardulais. Also further north at Llandovery at the junction of the A40 and A48 main roads. Look for the sign of the Welsh dragon at Carmarthen and west of here at Narberth, Kilgetty; further north at Llandilo and Newcastle Emlyn; and on the north coast at Cardigan.

There is a free trade which includes London and the home counties, where canned beer is supplied by J.T. Davies, wholesalers of Croydon.

BEERS

Draught   Bitter. A beer with a pleasant malty flavour.
Double Dragon. A strong draught bitter
Mild. A well-flavoured darkish mild.

Bottled	Bitter Ale. A pale ale.
	Pale ale. A little stronger.
	Nut Brown Ale. Not too sweet.
	John Brown. A stronger and sweeter brown ale.
Canned	Double Dragon. The draught DD in can.
	Double Strong. A very strong pale ale.

Draught beers are dispensed mainly by a top pressure system which is controlled to prevent the beer becoming carbonated. A few houses still have bar pumps or serve direct from the cask.

28   FULLER, SMITH & TURNER LTD

'The Beers with the Fuller Flavour'

ADDRESS

The Griffin Brewery, Chiswick, London, W4. Tel 01-994-7656.

The Brewery is between the river Thames and the A4, just before the start of the M4.

RECOGNITION

Usually 'Fullers' is written in white or other colours on the pub wall, or occasionally 'Fuller, Smith & Turner Ltd', and some pubs have pictorial signs. For the future the majority of Fuller houses are to have a brown facia on which is written the pub's name in white and 'Fullers' in yellow. In addition, some houses have wall boards usually at ground-floor level. These are painted orange with the Griffin and 'Fullers' in brown and the name of the house in white. At present, wall plaques are blue with a red Griffin but these are being changed to orange with similar colour schemes to the wall boards.

TIED HOUSES

There are just over 100 of these centred at Chiswick, Brentford and Ealing. They also extend along and within a line drawn between Hammersmith, Richmond, Hampton, Hayes, Hillingdon, Harrow and Acton. There are outposts at Wotton on the Dorking-Guildford road (Wotton Hatch Hotel), Croydon (Windmill Road and Isheldon Street), Peckham (Bird in Bush Road), Lewisham (Rennel Street), Shepherd's Bush (Melina Road), Kensington (Church St, North End Rd, Warwick Rd), Uxbridge (the Packet Boat at Cowley) and Staines (at the Hythe). Also nearer central London at St John's Wood (the Rossetti in Queen's Grove) and in Belgrave Mews West (Star Tavern).

There is a flourishing free club trade within the above area.

BEERS

Draught   London Pride.
                Bitter.
                    London Pride is the stronger of these two draught bitters, both of which have a pleasant distinctive flavour.
                Extra Special Bitter (ESB). A very strong beer, available in about a quarter of the houses.
                Hock Mild. A darkish mild.

Bottled   Light Ale.
               London Pride. The equivalent of the
               draught beer of the same name.
               Strong Ale. A strong dark beer.
               Golden Pride. A very strong bitter of
               barley wine strength.
               Brown Ale. The equivalent of Hock
               Mild.

The Bitter is conditioned before leaving the brewery
and sent out in cask as bright beer. The other three
are sent to the houses where they continue to
condition in cask. They are dispensed by the Porter
Lancastrian system in which there is a light covering
of CO_2 and the motive power is compressed air which
does not itself come into contact with the beer.

29   GEORGE GALE & CO LTD

'Gale's Ales'

ADDRESS

The Brewery, Horndean, Portsmouth, Hants. Tel
Horndean 2110 and 2177.

Horndean is a village a few miles north of
Portsmouth on the main London road.

The present brewery building, which is a con-
ventional tower brewery, was erected in 1869 after a
fire disaster had destroyed the earlier wooden
brewery a few years before. The original site of
brewing in Horndean was in the back premises of the
Ship & Bell public house, and although no traces are
left of the original brewery, the present sugar store
was at one time the Public House Tap.

Many Gale's pubs serve a large selection of wines based on old country recipes.

RECOGNITION

Usually 'Gale's Ales', 'Gale's Horndean Ales' or close variants are written on the wall of the pub. Sometimes there is an illuminated sign with 'Gale's Ales' in green letters and a white shield depicting a red unicorn on a green background. There is also a small green plaque alongside most of the pubs' doors with the unicorn in red.

TIED HOUSES

There are 88 of these, the majority of which are on or near the Portsmouth-London road (A3) as far north as Milford (Red Lion), or between this road, the Milford-Chichester road, and the coast between Chichester and Portsmouth. They are easily found in Chichester but a little harder to find in Portsmouth and Southsea (Cox's Hotel, Charlotte St; India Arms, Southsea; Mile End Cellars, Commercial Rd; Moncks Bar, High St; Ship & Castle, The Hard; Sociable Plover, Paulsgrove; Still & West, Bath Sq). Gale's pubs are also in Hayling Island (Kittiwake, Life-Boat Inn, Maypole Inn). Gale's beers can be found in Southampton (in New Road and Megesson Avenue) and several nearby towns and villages (Hamble, Bursledon, Fareham, Wickham, Curdridge, Dundridge) and also many villages and towns within this area. There are outposts as follows.

West of Winchester. At Braishfield and Longstock.
New Alresford district. At Bighton and Totford.

Near Alton. At Chawton and East Worldham.

Farnham town centre. Queen's Head.

Aldershot. In Grosvenor Road.

Near Guildford. At Shalford.

At or near Brighton. In King's Road (Harrison's Bars), at Binsted near Arundel, and Sompting near Lancing (Ball Tree Inn).

In the Isle of Wight. At Ryde (High Street and Simeon Street), and Sandown (St John's Road).

Much further north, beyond Reading. At Cane End and Mapledurham.

There is a free trade in the above areas.

BEER

Draught	Bitter. A pleasant and distinctive-flavoured brew.
	HSB—Best Bitter. Stronger and a little sweeter.
	Light Mild. More like a light bitter and not in all houses.
	Dark Mild.
	XXXXX. An old ale for the winter.
Keg	Gale's Keg. Quite well flavoured for a keg beer and dispensed from an attractive barrel-shaped counter mounting.
Bottled	Pale Ale.
	Champion Ale.
	Tudor Pale Ale.
	These three are pale ales in ascending order of gravity.
	Prize Old Ale. A very strong beer (barley wine) which is matured in cask and bottle for at least eighteen months and

has a unique flavour.

Nut Brown Ale. Medium sweet.

Nourishing Stout. A sweet stout.

Draught beers are dispensed by manual bar pumps or an electric metering system, at present mainly from wooden casks.

30   GIBBS, MEW & CO LTD

'Gibbs Beers'
'Gibbus Gibbs Great Beer'

ADDRESS

Anchor Brewery, Salisbury, Wilts. Tel 29244.

Salisbury, an attractive market city 23 miles north-west of Southampton, is the principal town of Wiltshire. It has a cathedral which is famous for having the tallest spire in England (405 ft) which is quite a landmark from outside the city.

RECOGNITION

Blue inn-signs with the name in white letters. Generally 'A Gibbs House' is written on the sign or pub wall.

TIED HOUSES

There are 50-60 of these centred in Salisbury and in many of the surrounding towns and villages. They cover a large part of Wiltshire, East Dorset and into Hampshire including as far east as behind Portsmouth on the top road to Fareham (the Churchillian at Cosham); and Ryde in the Isle of Wight (Ship & Castle). Gibbs beers are also to be found further north-west into Somerset at Frome (Wheatsheaf), Whatley (Sun Inn), and Bath (Angel, County Wine Vaults and Royal Oak at Widcombe). In north-west Wiltshire there is a Gibbs house at Melksham (The Board) and one at Corsham (Methuen Arms). West of Salisbury into Dorset look for the blue sign near Shaftesbury (at Donhead, Semley and Tisbury) and in Blandford (White Hart). The south-western outpost is at Dawlish in Devon (Grand Hotel).

There is a free trade in the same counties served from depots in Swindon and Sherborne; and in Oxfordshire, Middlesex, Surrey and Sussex served from a depot in Camberley.

BEERS

Keg   Special PA
                  Blue Keg.
                  Anchor Keg.
                  These are all well balanced keg bitters in ascending order of gravity—Anchor Keg is the strongest.
                  Super Mild. A sweet, dark mild ale.
Bottled   Light Ale.
                  Sarum Special. A high gravity pale ale.
                  Brown Ale.
                  Extra Stout. A medium sweet stout.

In addition, one or other of the following draught (keg) lagers can be obtained in Gibbs houses: Carlsberg, Tuborg, Harp or D.A.B. (Dortmunder). Keg beers are dispensed by top pressure CO_2.

31   GRAY & SONS (BREWERS) LTD

ADDRESS

7 Springfield Road, Chelmsford, Essex. Tel 52214.

Chelmsford is 32 miles north-east of London just off the A12. The brewery is right in the town centre almost opposite Woolworths, behind which there is a car park.

RECOGNITION

There is no particular colour or pattern, pubs being fairly inconspicuously distinguished by 'Gray & Sons' on the wall or sign.

TIED HOUSES

Most of the 52 licensed houses are in and around Chelmsford and Maldon and villages between, and towards the coast. They can be found as follows.

In and around Chelmsford. 11 in Chelmsford, including Springfield, and easy to find; at Widford to the south (Sir Evelyn Wood); Galleywood (Horse & Groom); and Writtle (Wheatsheaf).

West of Chelmsford. At Ingatestone (Star), Mill Green, Kelvedon Hatch, Stondon Massey, Ongar (Cock Tavern), and Brentwood (Victoria on Ongar road).

At Billericay. Railway, Coach & Horses, and nearby at South Green (Duke of York).

Near Southend. At Westcliff-on-Sea (Cricketers).

Between the rivers Blackwater and Crouch. At Mundon Hill, Steeple, Tillingham, Althorne, South-

minster and Burnham-on-Crouch (New Welcome
Sailor, Queens Head, Victoria).

Maldon district. At Maldon (Carpenters Arms,
Queens Head, Royal Oak, Borough Arms, Queen
Victoria, Swan Hotel), Heybridge, Woodham Mortimer, Woodham Walter, Danbury, Boreham and Hatfield Peverel.

Further east. At Feering, Tiptree, Tolleshunt Major
and Tolleshunt D'Arcy.

North of Halstead. At Castle Hedingham and Sible
Hedingham.

BEERS

Draught   Bitter. A well-flavoured, distinctive brew
            with the smack of hops.
            Best Bitter. Stronger than the 'ordinary'.
            Mild. A dark beer.
            Stock. A pleasant, fairly strong, darkish
            drink which is roughly a cross between
            the bitter and the mild.
Bottled   Light Ale.
            Brown Ale.
            Home Brew. This is the Stock in bottle.
Draught beers are dispensed from the wood direct or
by manual bar pumps.

32   GREENALL, WHITLEY & CO LTD

'Smile please, you are in Greenall Whitley land'

ADDRESS

Wilderspool Brewery, Warrington, Lancs. Tel 35111.
    Warrington is an ancient town on the north bank

of the river Mersey noted for foundries, chemicals, soapworks, and brewing.

Greenall, Whitley operate two other breweries—in nearby St Helens, and in Wem, which is further south, in Shropshire.

RECOGNITION

The company emblem is a red oval with a white border and with a notch on each side. Inside the red part is depicted a yellowish-gold goddess blowing a hunting horn. This is either as an illuminated sign, or itself on a square green signboard with the name of the pub in white and 'Greenall Whitley' in yellow. Instead of dark green, sometimes the sign is a bright yellow, especially in south-west Lancashire, but the yellow signs are rapidly being replaced by green ones.

TIED HOUSES

There are nearly 1,500 licensed houses covering a wide area in the north-west and west as follows.

In Lancashire. The majority are in the south-west of the county, up as far as Preston and Blackpool and to Manchester in the east.

In Cheshire and Shropshire. Well spread out over both counties and easy to find.

In Derbyshire. At Chapel-en-le-Frith in the Peak district.

In Staffordshire. At Armitage (between Stafford and Lichfield) and at Blackshaw Moor in the north.

In Herefordshire. At Tenbury Wells.

In North Wales. Spread out over Anglesey, Caernarvonshire, Denbighshire, Flintshire, Merionethshire and Montgomeryshire.

There is also a string of eighteen 'Compass' hotels, nearly all of which are residential.

A Greenall Whitley guide to pubs and hotels called 'Pub Pleasure' can be obtained from the brewery.

BEERS

Draught	Best Bitter. A well-balanced bitter.
	Pale Ale. A light mild similar to a bitter.
	Mild. A full-bodied dark mild.
Keg	Festival Keg. A keg bitter.
	Draught Grunhalle. A high-gravity lager.
Bottled	Champion Ale. A pale ale.
	Festival Export Ale. A strong light ale. Not the same as the keg.
	Five Star Strong Ale. A barley wine nip.
	Old Chester Ale. A dark and sweet, strong 'Old' ale.
	Bullseye Brown Ale. A medium sweet brown ale.
	Family Ale. A sweet brown ale.
	Red Rose Stout. A sweet stout.
	Grunhalle Lager.

Draught beers are dispensed by electric pumps, top pressure or in some cases by manual bar pumps.

33a   GREENE, KING & SONS LTD

'Real Draught Beer'

ADDRESS

Westgate Brewery, Bury St Edmunds, Suffolk. Tel 3371.

Bury St Edmunds is an ancient market town in West Suffolk, 28 miles east of Cambridge.

There are two subsidiary breweries:

Greene, King (Biggleswade) Ltd (33b), The Brewery, Biggleswade, Bedfordshire. Tel 2251.

Rayment & Co Ltd (33c), Furneux Pelham, Buntingford, Herts. Tel Brent Pelham 254. Rayment & Co is a small country brewery which brews independently but also supplies many of the Greene King group beers.

Greene, King & Sons Ltd

RECOGNITION

'Greene King' is written on the pub's wall or at the bottom of the sign. The house mark is a head of a green king outlined in green and is derived from the whole figure. A relief plaque of the complete king is still to be seen on the outside wall of the pubs. The name originates from two breweries of those names.

TIED HOUSES

There are almost 900 of these and they extend over East Anglia and adjoining counties north of London. They can be found from King's Lynn on the Wash, across to Norwich and throughout West Suffolk. They are hard to find in Norfolk, but include the following: Ostrich Inn, Castle Acre, King's Lynn; Wenns Hove, King's Lynn; Prince of Wales, South Gates, King's Lynn; Lord Nelson, Burnham Market; Crown, Colkirk, Fakenham; Vine, Fakenham; Albion, Thetford; in Norwich the Windmill in Plumstead

Road and White Cottage in Penn Grove (off Aylsham Road). Greene King houses are also in Cambridge, Huntingdon, Northampton, Wellingborough, Bedford, Luton, Dunstable and in the country around those towns. In Essex they can be found from Colchester to the surroundings of Witham, Braintree and Chelmsford. In Hertfordshire in some of the villages in the north of the county and south to Hertford. Outposts are in Barnet (Builders Arms in Albert Rd), Chorleywood (White Horse), Rickmansworth (Coach & Horses), Croxley Green (Fox & Hounds), Watford (Nascot Arms, Estcourt Tavern) and Abbots Langley (Swan in College Rd).

The Nutshell in the centre of Bury St Edmunds is one of the smallest pubs in the country and is reputed to have the smallest bar.

There is an extensive free trade.

BEERS

The speciality of the company is its draught beer range on which its reputation is largely founded. Including Rayment's beers, there are eight draught beers and four keg beers.

Draught	IPA Bitter. A draught bitter with a good hop rate.
	IA Light Bitter. A lighter bitter mainly in and around Bury St Edmunds and Sudbury.
	Light Mild. Also a light bitter but not quite so bitter as IA or IPA. Mostly in Biggleswade area and points west.
	XX Mild. A dark mild.
	Abbot Ale. A strong, robust bitter.
Keg	King Keg. A keg bitter.

Polar. A light coloured, chilled beer for the summer.

Bottled   Pale Ale.

Crown Ale. A medium gravity, mellow pale ale.

Abbot Ale. A strong pale ale.

St Edmund's Ale. The strongest of the pale ales, brewed to commemorate St Edmund's martyrdom, and still continued.

Harvest Ale. A sweet, dark beer.

Burton Ale. Dark but less sweet.

Suffolk Ale. A strong, dark and well-flavoured beer.

Farm Stout. A sweet stout.

Audit Ale. A barley wine.

Draught beers are sometimes dispensed direct from wooden or metal casks, or by manual bar pumps, but the top pressure system is now the most widely used.

33c   RAYMENT & CO LTD

'Your country brewery'

RECOGNITION

'Rayment's Pelham Ales' is written in a red strip below the inn sign picture or sometimes on a green sign. 'Rayment's of Pelham' may be written on the pub wall.

TIED HOUSES

There are 31 licensed houses, mainly in the countryside around Bishop's Stortford and Saffron Walden as follows.

In the villages west of the A11. At Furneux Pelham itself (2), at Albury, Arkesden, Barkway, Hunsdon (the 'Crazy Pub'—open only in busy periods, and only couples admitted), Little Hadham, Meesden, Wareside, Wicken Bonhunt, and as far west as Tewin near Welwyn Garden City.

In Bishop's Stortford and nearby. In Bishop's Stortford there are 4 (Cellarman, Havers Lane; Rose & Crown, Evavion Road; Three Tuns, London Road; Wheatsheaf, Rye Street), with others in Birchangar, Harlow (Willow Beauty, Hodings Road), Hatfield Heath, Sawbridgeworth and Stansted (Cock, Silver Street; Dog & Duck, Lower Street; Ash, Burton End).

In and around Saffron Walden. In Saffron Walden (Gate, Thaxted Road; Victory, Little Walden Road; Axe & Compasses, Radwinter Road); others at Clavering (Waggon & Horses), Debden, Duxford, Newport, Radwinter and Thaxted (Butcher's Arms).

There is a substantial free trade which accounts for some 70 per cent of the business. It runs from Bishop's Stortford south to London where it is mainly in the east, north-east and West End. It includes places such as Brentwood, Enfield and Southgate.

BEERS

Draught	BBA Bitter. A well hopped 'beery' beer of pleasant distinctive flavour.
	AK Pale Ale. A light mild not unlike the bitter.
	XX Mild. A dark mild.

Keg	Keg Bitter.
	Keg Mild (Dagger).
	These two are not in all the pubs.
Bottled	Pelham. A light ale.
	Super Ale. A strong light ale.
	Brown Ale. Medium sweet.
	Dagger Brown. Sweeter and darker.

Greene King beers such as Farm Stout, Audit, Abbot Ale, Suffolk Ale and St Edmund's Ale are usually on sale in Rayment houses.

Because of the increasing popularity of Rayment's draught beers, production at Furneux Pelham is to be concentrated on these. All or most of the bottled beers would then be supplied by Greene King who have adequate bottling capacity for both companies.

Draught beers are dispensed by manual bar pumps or direct from wooden or metal casks, but top pressure is being introduced.

34   THE GUERNSEY BREWERY CO (1920) LTD

'Pony Ales'

ADDRESS

South Esplanade, St Peter Port, Guernsey, Channel Isles. Tel 20143.

Guernsey is unique in that the brewers do not advertise on their own pubs, and usually only the name of the pub is to be seen. Guernsey enjoys self-government and beer is cheaper than in the United Kingdom.

RECOGNITION

A very few pubs have an inconspicuous 'Pony Ales' written on the outside, and mostly there is no brewer's sign. The exception is the Pony Inn at Les Cappelles, which is the most modern in the island.

TIED HOUSES

There are around 40-50, but most of the trade is via free outlets. The company also supplies Alderney, Herm and Sark on free trade.

BEERS

Draught	Mild. A medium dark mild which is dry hopped.
Keg	Pony Keg Bitter. A well hopped, high gravity keg beer. Guinness and Harp Lager are both available in kegs.
Bottled	Pony IPA. A pale ale similar to the keg bitter. Pony Ale. The mild in bottle. Pony Brown Ale. Not too sweet. Full-bodied and fairly heavily primed. Milk Stout. Medium sweet.

Guinness and Harp Lager are both bottled at the brewery.

The keg bitter is dispensed by top pressure and the mild by manual bar pumps or direct from the cask.

35   HALL & WOODHOUSE LTD

'Badger Beers'

ADDRESS

The Brewery, Blandford Forum, Dorset. Tel Blandford 2141.

Blandford is a pleasant market town on the river Stour with many eighteenth-century buildings.

The brewery stands on the south bank of the river between Blandford Forum and the adjoining village of Blandford St Mary. Hall & Woodhouse have been Dorset brewers since 1777, first at Ansty a few miles west of Blandford, and then at Blandford itself since 1882.

RECOGNITION

Hall & Woodhouse pubs are easily spotted because nearly all have a wall finish of an off-white 'Rogstone' produced specially for the Blandford brewery. A distinctive 'Badger Blue' is often used on doors and sills. Illuminated signs depicting a badger and 'Badger Ales' or 'Badger Beers' hang above one of the doors. 'Hall & Woodhouse' and 'Badger Beers' are usually written on the pub's wall. Most pubs also have pictorial signs on a Badger Blue background with the pub's name above the picture and 'Hall & Woodhouse' written below.

TIED HOUSES

There are about 250 of these covering the counties of

Dorset, West Hampshire and parts of Somerset and Wiltshire. The majority are country pubs in the rolling Dorset countryside. A map giving information about all the pubs can be obtained from the brewery, and this shows that 'Badger territory' mainly occupies an area bounded by a line from Salisbury through Ringwood to Bournemouth in the east; from Wincanton through Sherborne to Weymouth (where there are Badger pubs in King St and Maiden St) in the west; from Poole to Weymouth in the south; and from Wincanton through Mere to Salisbury in the north. Within this area they are easy to find and many provide food and accommodation. There are outposts at Hillhead near Lee-on-Solent (the Osborne View); at Swanage (Mowlem); at Clevedon on the Somerset coast between Bristol and Weston-super-Mare (Regent); at Lymington (the Londes-borough); and at Walkford near Christchurch (the Amberwood). Some of these are steakhouses and there are also steakhouses at Salisbury and Bourne-mouth (Fir Vale Rd).

The free trade extends from Southampton to Taunton.

BEERS

Draught	Bitter. Well hopped and of a pleasant distinctive character. Often called locally the 'Boy's Bitter'.
	Best Bitter. Similar but of a higher gravity, less bitter and more body.
	Mild. A dark beer.
Keg	Badger Bright. The Bitter in keg form.
	Forum Keg. The Best Bitter in keg form.
	Brock Lager. Brewed in Blandford.

Bottled   Badger Light Ale.
           Forum Pale Ale. A high gravity pale ale
           of 'export' quality.
           Badger XXXX Old English Ale. A strong
           dark 'Old' Ale.
           Stingo Barley Wine.
           Badger Stout. Medium sweet.
           Badger John Brown. Sweeter and of
           higher gravity.
           Brock Lager. The 'draught' lager in
           bottle.
Cans   Badger Bright, Badger Brown Ale and
           Brock Lager are all available in 10 oz
           cans. The Badger Bright is also in 5 pint
           cans. Canned beers can be obtained
           through Littlewood's Mail Order House
           and these are Gold Medal Export (the
           Forum Keg in can), John Brown, Export
           Stout and Brock Lager. They are all in
           12 oz cans.

Draught beers are dispensed by means of top pressure, electric pumps (in bigger houses with deep
cellars), manual bar pumps and in a few cases direct
from the cask.

36   HARDYS AND HANSONS LTD

'Stop with the hop'

ADDRESS

Kimberley Brewery, Kimberley, Nottingham. Tel
Kimberley 3611.

Kimberley is a small town 6 miles north-west of Nottingham and 1½ miles from the M1. Main industries are knitwear, lingerie and brewing.

RECOGNITION

A hanging or post sign with a conspicuous yellow hop points the way to Kimberley Ales. The sign carries the names 'Hardy Hanson' and attached is the name of the pub. 'Hardys Kimberley Ale Hanson' (with 'Kimberley Ale' in oblique script) is often on a painted or neon sign, usually green but sometimes other colours.

TIED HOUSES

About 230 of these, with the greatest concentration in the triangle formed by the towns of Nottingham, Derby and Chesterfield. Apart from these towns, Kimberley Ales can also be found as far off as Buxton, Doncaster, Skegness, Coningsby (Lincs), and Leicester. There is a free trade in the area of tied houses.

BEERS

Draught	Best Bitter. A well hopped beer with a bitter, malty flavour.
	Mild. A dark beer.
Keg	KK. A keg beer with some of the Bitter flavour and with a smoother and less well-defined palate.
Bottled	Guinea Gold. A light ale.
	Starbright IPA. A stronger pale ale.

Old Kim. A strong ale.
Special Brown Ale. A medium sweet nut brown ale.
Blackamoor Stout. A sweet stout.

Draught beers are dispensed by electric pumps and in some cases manual bar pumps.

37   HARTLEYS' (ULVERSTON) LTD

ADDRESS

The Old Brewery, Ulverston, Lancs. Tel 53269 and 52610.

Ulverston is a small market town with a cattle auction every Thursday, when the pubs are open all day. It lies in the Furness peninsula—a piece of land jutting out into the Irish Sea south of the Lake District. It has an anti-biotics factory and at one time iron ore was mined here. Not very far from Ulverston—at Swarthmoor Hall—George Fox founded the Quaker religion. (The date on the chimney stack of the brewery is 1754, and from then to the present day the Old Brewery has been quenching the local thirsts.)

RECOGNITION

The pubs all display conspicuous peacock-blue sign boards with usually the name of the pub and underneath 'Hartleys Prize Ales' all in white letters.

TIED HOUSES

The peacock-blue signs can be seen throughout the

Lake District as well as in the Furness peninsula and nearby. Hartleys' houses can be found as follows.

In the Furness peninsula. At Barrow, Hawcoat, Dalton, Lindal, Swarthmoor, Urswick, Stainton, Baycliff and Ulverston.

In Furness but just north of the peninsula and in the hills. At Penny Bridge, Lowick and Oxen Park.

To the east in Cartmel peninsula. At Flookburgh, Cartmell and Lindale.

On the A6. At Milnthorpe and further south at Yealand Conyers just off the A6 and at Lancaster (Waggon & Horses).

In Cumberland. At Cleator Moor (New Crown) and Millom.

In the Lake District. At Coniston (Crown, Ship), Bowness (Albert, New Hall), Ambleside (Unicorn, Golden Rule, Outgate Inn which is between Ambleside and Hawkshead), Hawkshead (Queen's Head) and at Kendal (Sawyers' Arms, White Hart).

Hartleys is one of the few small breweries which supply draught beer to a major group, and many of the pubs in the area sell Hartleys' beers. There is a free trade to clubs throughout Lakeland as well as the peninsula.

BEERS

Draught	Bitter. A well-balanced brew.
	XB. A well hopped strong bitter—OG of 1041. The name stems from past history. It was a symbol used to distinguish beers destined for the pubs of Thompson of Barrow who were supplied by Hartleys before they sold out to a major group.
	Mild. Dark and well hopped. Not too sweet.

Draught Guinness is in the pubs, and certain houses in the Lake District have Whitbread Tankard. Heineken Lager is in most of the pubs.

Bottled   These are supplied by Whitbread. Guinness is bottled at the brewery.

Draught beers are dispensed by manual bar pumps or electric pumps. Pubs that have electric pumps also retain the bar pumps, for their attractive appearance, and in case of a power cut they can be brought back into use.

38   HARVEY & SON (LEWES) LTD

'Draught Sussex Bitter'

Note See also under 7 Beard & Co (Lewes) Ltd, whose pubs sell Harvey's beers.

ADDRESS

Bridge Wharf Brewery, Lewes, Sussex. Tel 3126.

Lewes is the county town of Sussex and is a few miles from Brighton.

RECOGNITION

Usually 'Harvey & Son' is written on the pub's wall, or just 'Harveys'. Sometimes 'Noted Ales, Wines and Spirits'. 'Draught Sussex Bitter sold here' is written on an orange plaque on an outside wall.

TIED HOUSES

There are 24 which extend over most of East Sussex

with the largest number in one town at Eastbourne where there are 5 (Arlington Arms, Terminus Hotel, Victoria Hotel, Hurst Arms, Lambe Inn in the Old Town). On or near the London road out of Eastbourne there are Harvey houses at Stone Cross, Polegate, Hailsham (Grenadier, King's Head), Chiddingly, East Hoathly and Uckfield (Alma Arms). Then to the east at Blackboys, Magham Down and Boreham Street. Towards Lewes look for the Harvey sign at Berwick and Glynde and at Lewes itself the Swan Inn. Then to the north at Isfield and north-west at Plumpton. Northern outposts are at Crawley (White Hart), Turners Hill, Withyham and Bells Yew Green (just south of Tunbridge Wells).

BEERS

Draught	Bitter. A nutty flavoured draught beer which is not in all the houses. Best Bitter. Stronger and a little sweeter. Mild. A pleasant dry dark mild. XXXX (Old). A strong dark ale. Elizabethan Ale. A draught barley wine, very strong and satisfying. Not in all houses and mainly in winter.
Keg	Keg Bitter. The Best Bitter in container.
Bottled	IPA. A pale ale. Blue Label. A stronger pale ale. Nut Brown. A medium sweet brown ale. Exhibition Brown. Stronger than the Nut Brown. Sweet Stout. Elizabethan Ale. Barley wine corresponding to the draught.

A top pressure system and manual bar pumps are both in use to dispense draught beers.

39   HIGSONS BREWERY LTD

ADDRESS

127 Dale Street, Liverpool, Lancs. Tel 236-1255.

Higsons have been independent brewers on Merseyside since 1780, and the brewery is in Stanhope Street near the docks.

RECOGNITION

The trade mark is a circular red plaque with an oast-house in black and white in which is the 'liver bird' of Liverpool in black. The city coat of arms is based on the mythical liver bird which may have been the eagle of St John—King John having granted Liverpool its first charter in 1207. The plaque may be fixed on the wall of the pub. The pubs can also be recognised by white barrel-shaped illuminated signs with the trade mark in the middle.

TIED HOUSES

There are about 130 managed, and 30 tenanted houses, mostly in the Merseyside area of Liverpool but also radiating out from the centre of the city in all directions. There is one in the centre of Manchester (in Crown Square) and in Rochdale in Baillie St, and Higsons' beers may be drunk in Wallasey and north along the coast as far as Southport, Blackpool and Fleetwood. Also at Chester (eg Bull & Stirrup) and in the Potteries where Higsons' beers can be found at Stoke (Glebe), Hanley (Albion, Trumpet) and Newcastle (Bull's Vaults). Also at Leek and nearby. In North Wales the pubs go as far along the coast as Holywell and Abergele.

There is a free trade within the area which includes British Legion clubs, rugby clubs, and both Liverpool and Everton football clubs.

BEERS

Draught	Bitter. A well-flavoured beer which is well hopped.
	Mild. A dark mild.
Keg	Bitter.
	Mild.
Bottled	Pale Ale.
	Double Top. A brown ale.
	Stingo Gold. A barley wine.
Cans	Home Pak. A 4½ gallon non-returnable container.
	Chota Keg. A 4 pint can.

Draught beers are dispensed by manual bar pumps or a metered top pressure system.

40   HOLDEN'S BREWERY LTD

'The Beer with the Glow'

ADDRESS

Hopden Brewery, Woodsetten, Dudley, Worcs. Tel Sedgley 2051/2.

Page 167 (*above*) This miniature brewery, now disused, once supplied the adjoining home-brewed pub (the Golden Lion, Southwick, Hants); (*below*) the traditional tower brewery at Hook Norton, Oxfordshire, still produces fine ales

Page 168 (*above*) A country brewery (Rayment & Co, Furneux Pelham, Herts); (*below*) a modern brewhouse at Blackburn, Lancs. (Daniel Thwaites & Co Ltd)

Woodsetten is two or three miles south-east of Wolverhampton towards Dudley.

RECOGNITION

'Edwin Holden's the Quality Beer' is usually written on the pub's wall. Other catch phrases in use are 'Holden's Golden', 'The Beer with the Glow' and 'Black Country Bitter'.

TIED HOUSES

These are at Woodsetten, Coseley, Daisy Bank, Bilston, Upper and Lower Gornal, West Bromwich and Brierley Hill.

There is also a free trade in a number of clubs in this area.

BEERS

Draught   Mild. A pleasant dark beer.
Keg   Golden Keg. A full-flavoured bitter which is chilled and filtered but not pasteurised.
Bottled   Park Ale. A dark mild.

The draught beer is dispensed by manual bar pumps and the keg beer by top pressure.

41   JOSEPH HOLT LTD

ADDRESS

Derby Brewery, Empire Street, Cheetham, Manchester 3, Lancs. Tel 061-834 3285/6.

RECOGNITION

Holt's houses may have 'Holt's' or 'Holt's Fine Ales' written on the wall of the pub; or in a very few cases there may be no sign at all other than the pub's name. New signboards are now gradually being displayed on Holt's licensed houses; on them is written 'Holt's Manchester Ales'.

TIED HOUSES

There are just over 80 of these and they are distributed over Manchester and its close suburbs, but there are none right in the centre of the city. Concentrations are in Salford, Eccles, Whitefield and Prestwich, also other areas just to the north of Manchester such as Heaton Park.

BEERS

Draught	Bitter. A well-balanced traditional brew.
	Mild. A dark mild.
Bottled	Pale Ale.
	Six X. A barley wine.
	Diamond Ale. A strong brown ale.
	Brown Stout. Medium sweet.

Draught beers are dispensed by means of manual bar pumps or electric pumps.

42   HOME BREWERY CO LTD

'Home Ales'

ADDRESS

The Brewery, Mansfield Road, Daybrook, Notts. Tel Nottingham 26-8241.

Daybrook is on the northern outskirts of Nottingham, famous for its lace and hosiery manufacture. The river Trent passes through Nottingham which is nearly right in the centre of England. There is a castle, and the market place—not used now—is the largest in the county.

RECOGNITION

Normally by an illuminated sign decorated with the figure of Robin Hood in green and the words 'Home Ales' displayed in a conspicuous position. Many houses also have their own inn-signs indicating their names.

TIED HOUSES

There are over 400 licensed houses covering a wide area, extending from Nottingham through the counties of Derbyshire, Huntingdonshire, Leicestershire, Lincolnshire, Northamptonshire, Staffordshire, Yorkshire and Warwickshire. However, the majority are concentrated within fifty miles of the city centre.

BEERS

Draught	Bitter. A well hopped beer.
	Mild. A full, dark mild.
Keg	Five-Star. A high gravity keg beer.
Bottled	Robin Hood IPA. A strong pale ale.
	Bendigo. A strong ale.
	Home Brewed. A brown ale.
	Luncheon Ale. A lighter brown ale.
	Home Stout. A sweet stout.

Draught beers are delivered to the pubs either in cask or by tanker. They are dispensed in some cases by manual bar pumps, but increasingly by metering systems and electric pumps.

43   HOOK NORTON BREWERY CO LTD

'Hookey'

ADDRESS

Hook Norton, nr. Banbury, Oxfordshire. Tel Hook Norton 210.

The country lanes to the south-west of Banbury take one through the rolling North Oxfordshire countryside to the peaceful village of Hook Norton. The brewery, which was built on the traditional tower pattern, stands out prominently like an eastern castle, at one end of the village.

RECOGNITION

The pubs have conspicuous red signs with their name and 'Hook Norton Ales' written in gold letters. The house sign is a red barley sheaf.

TIED HOUSES

There are 34 of these in and around Hook Norton (where there are 4) and Banbury (2 here—in Butchers Row and Parsons St). North-east of Banbury, Hookey Ales can be found at Lower Boddington, Chipping

Warden, Great Bourton, Wardington, Thorpe Mande-
ville, Sulgrave, Marston St Lawrence, Greatworth and
Warkworth. They can also be found further south at
King's Sutton, Aynho, Deddington, Stoke Lyne and
Chipping Norton (Albion Tavern, Red Lion). Around
Hook Norton but mostly on the north side the red
signs can be seen in the villages of Whichford,
Wigginton, Bloxham, Brailes (2), Edge Hill, Epwell
and Balscote. Outposts are at Leamington Spa (in
Princes St), Abthorpe which is just south-west of
Towcester, Woodstock (The Queen's Own, rather
inconspicuous on the main through road without its
red sign), Moreton-in-Marsh (The Wellington), and
north-east of here at Paxford.

There is a strong free trade as far apart as Oxford,
Coventry, Thame and Chinnor (out on the Thame
road).

BEERS

Draught	Best Bitter. A draught bitter with the smack of hops.
	Hookey. A light mild with an agreeable flavour.
Bottled	Jack Pot. The bitter in bottle.
	Hook Ale. The mild in bottle.
	Brown Ale.

Draught beers are dry-hopped and are dispensed by
manual bar pumps. A few houses use top pressure and
so does the free trade.

44   T. HOSKINS LTD

'Have a drink at home'

ADDRESS

Beaumanor Road, Leicester. Tel 61122.

T. Hoskins is unique in the brewing world in having its one tied house some distance away from the brewery. It is at Market Bosworth, which is ten miles due west of Leicester and lies just off the A447. Yet draught beer can also be obtained at the off-licence adjoining the brewery, dispensed into bottles to take away and drink at home. It is best to bring empty bottles for this.

TIED HOUSE

This is at Market Bosworth. The brewery's name is not on the pub, which displays no means of recognition other than its name—The Red Lion.

Hoskins also supply the free trade in the Leicester area and direct to private houses.

There is a second off-licence in Twycross St, Highfields, in Leicester, but it does not dispense draught beer.

BEERS

Draught	Bitter. A pleasant nutty-flavoured beer. Mild. A dark beer.
Bottled	Home brewed. A pale ale. IPA Bitter. Stronger than the last. It is the bitter in bottle. Strong. A strong dark ale. Best Mild. The mild in bottle. Nut Brown. A brown ale which is stronger than the mild.

Cans	Bitter and mild in 7 pint cans.
Casks	Draught bitter and mild in 4½, 6 and 9 gallon cans.
Keg	Keg bitter and mild in 9 gallon kegs.

Draught beer is dispensed via bar pumps.

45 THE HULL BREWERY CO LTD

'The sign of good ale'

ADDRESS

Anchor Brewery, Silvester St, Hull, Yorks. Tel 36961.

The brewery's dray-horses are a picturesque sight in the town as they take the beer on local deliveries. The brewery owns five Clydesdales, the breed it has used for many years.

RECOGNITION

The 'sign of good ale' is an anchor which may be seen outside some of the pubs. These appear in black and white with yellow doors. They have pictorial house signs in the country and beehive-shaped signs in the towns. Many of the older signs are still to be seen and Hull Brewery houses can also be recognised by green square signs depicting the anchor house sign. Also written outside the pubs may be 'an HB house', 'Hull Brewery' or 'a Hull Brewery House'.

TIED HOUSES

There are 200 of these, 79 of which are in Hull itself. The houses fall in an area bounded by Scarborough,

Pontefract, Scunthorpe, Brigg and the East Yorkshire coast. There are also scattered outposts at Conisborough (between Doncaster and Rotherham) and between Brigg and Grimsby.

There is a free trade beyond the above area to include Doncaster, Whitby and Malton areas.

BEERS

Draught	Bitter. A well-balanced and fairly bitter draught beer.
	Light Mild. Could be described as a light bitter. To be found mainly in the West Riding.
	Mild. A dark beer.
Keg	Keg Bitter. Less bitter than the draught bitter and not in all the pubs.
	Top Score. A 'draught' lager which has been recently introduced.
Bottled	Light Ale.
	Pale Ale. Stronger and lighter in colour than the light ale.
	Mild. A dark mild in bottle which is sold much lighter in colour in the West Riding.
	Brown Ale. Sweeter and stronger than the mild ales.
	Anchor Export. Stronger than the pale ale.
	Double Anchor. The strongest pale ale, of a barley wine type.
Canned	The Light, Brown, Anchor Export and Top Score Lager can be obtained in cans and there is a Mini Keg containing 7 pints.

Draught beers are dispensed by the Porter-Lancastrian system, with plastic bags and counter meters in which the beer is raised by compressed air, also by manual beer engine bar pumps, as it is found that many people prefer their beer to be drawn in this way.

46   HYDES' ANVIL BREWERY LTD

'Hydes' Anvil Ales'

ADDRESS

Anvil Brewery, 46 Moss Lane West, Manchester, Lancs. Tel 061-226 1317.

The brewery is named after its trade mark, an anvil. It is an independent family company and can trace its origins back to 1863 although it was known to exist before that date. It moved to the present brewery in 1898 prior to which operations had been from breweries in the Ardwick and Rusholme districts of Manchester.

RECOGNITION

Hydes' Anvil houses can usually be identified by 'Hydes' Anvil Ales' or 'Anvil Ales' being written on the wall of the pub.

TIED HOUSES

There are up to 50 of these spread over Manchester but mostly south of the city centre, close to which there is one—in Portland Street. There are also some Hydes' houses south of Chester, nearly all of which are in North Wales to the west of Wrexham. Hydes' beer in this area can be found at Rhydtalog (Liver), Bwlchgwyn (Kings Head), Summerhill (Crown), Cymmau (Ye Olde Talbot), Moss (Bird in Hand) and Bersham (Black Lion). There is a Hydes' house to the east of Wrexham at Broxton on the Nantwich road (Royal Oak).

Building will shortly commence on two new pubs and there are a good number of off-licences.

There is also an active free trade.

BEERS

Draught	Bitter. A well hopped draught beer.
	Mild Ale. A dark beer.
	Best Mild. A blend between the Bitter and the Mild.
Keg	Anvil Keg Bitter. With some character.
	Amboss Draught Lager.
Bottled	Anvil Ale. A pale ale.
	Anvil Gold. A strong pale ale.
	Anvil Strong Ale. A strong dark ale.
	Anvil Brown Ale.
	Anvil Stout. A sweet Stout.

Draught beers are mostly dispensed through metered dispensers in conjunction with electric cellar motors, but manual bar pumps are still in use.

47   JENNINGS BROTHERS LTD

'Castle Ales'

ADDRESS

The Castle Brewery, Cockermouth, Cumberland. Tel 3214.

Cockermouth is a small West Cumberland town surrounded by hills and placed at the junction of the rivers Cocker and Derwent. It is where William Wordsworth was born and also Fletcher Christian of 'Mutiny on the Bounty' fame. There is an old castle which is quite near to the brewery.

Jennings Bros Ltd was registered in 1887 and at first there were two breweries, one being at nearby Lorton where the original maltings were. The present brewhouse—just below the castle—is at the apex of the junction of the rivers Cocker and Derwent. The maltings are close by, and the water for brewing is drawn from a 70-foot well.

RECOGNITION

Usually an illuminated sign on which is written 'Castle Ales' in blue letters with a picture of a castle and some green bushes, below which is written 'Jennings Bros Ltd'. There may be a hanging pictorial sign with 'A Jennings House' below the picture. Or 'Jennings Bros Ltd' may be written on the pub's wall.

TIED HOUSES

There are 79 of these in Cockermouth and the surrounding towns and villages of West Cumberland— eg Wigton, Maryport, Workington, Whitehaven, Egremont, Keswick and many points between. Further afield Castle Ales can be found at Penrith just off the M6 (Salutation Hotel) and southwards near the coast road between Egremont and Millom at Drigg (Station Hotel).

Free trade is in the above area and extends as far as Silloth on the Solway Firth.

BEERS

Draught	Bitter. A well hopped brew
	Mild. A dark beer.
Keg	KB Keg Bitter. A high-gravity, well-flavoured keg beer which is not over-gassed.
Bottled	Special Pale Ale.
	Castle Pale Ale. A stronger pale ale—the equivalent of the draught bitter.
	Export. The strongest of the pale ales.
	Brown Ale. Medium sweet.

Draught beers are dispensed by means of manual bar pumps or electric pumps.

48   JPS BREWERIES LTD

'Simpkiss home brewed'

ADDRESS

Dennis Brewery, Brettell Lane, Brierley Hill, Staffs. Tel 77576.

Brierley Hill is in the rolling hills of the Black Country—which is not without its character—about 12 miles west of Birmingham.

RECOGNITION

Look out for red inn-signs or the name 'Simpkiss' in red letters. The inn's name is usually in gold letters. Some houses advertise 'Simpkiss's home brewed'—JPS Breweries originated and grew up from a home-brewed house forty years or more ago.

TIED HOUSES

There are 17 of these covering a radius of 5-10 miles from Brierley Hill and as far as the Wolverhampton-Walsall road in the north of the area. They can be found in Brierley Hill itself (Brettell Lane, Amblecote Road, Church Street, Silver End and Dudley Road); Lye (Balds Lane); Upper Gornal (Clarence Street); Lower Gornal (Himley Road); Kingswinford (Greensforge and Summer Street); Wallheath (Hinksford and Albdon Street); Stourbridge (Bridgnorth Road); Cradley Heath (Upper High Street); Kinver (Stone Lane); and Willenhall (Somerford Place and Stafford Street).

One-third of the trade is via free outlets.

BEERS

Draught	Best Bitter. A well hopped brew with a good flavour.
	Mild. A dark mild.
	Old Ale. A strong dark ale brewed from October to March.
Keg	Keg Bitter. Introduced in 1972 and distinctively flavoured.
Bottled	Extra Special Bitter. The Best Bitter conditioned and bottled.
	Old Ale. The draught OA in bottle. Winter only.
	Nut Brown. Brown ale.

Draught beers are dispensed by manual bar pumps or electric pumps.

49   KING & BARNES LTD

'Horsham Ales'

ADDRESS

18, Bishopric, Horsham, Sussex. Tel 61484/5.

Horsham is a Mid-Sussex market town about 30 miles south of London.

RECOGNITION

Conspicuous red inn-signs with gold lettering or sign paintings framed in red point the way to King & Barnes' 'Fine Horsham Ales'.

TIED HOUSES

You can drink 'Horsham Ales' in 58 pubs which are easy to find in Horsham and surrounding villages. Further out a little more detective work is needed. Outposts are at Reigate (Nutley Hall), Leigh and Blackbrook (near Dorking) in Surrey, to the north; Eridge near Tunbridge Wells (Huntsman), near Lindfield (Snowdrop) and Ardingly (Avins Bridge), to the east; Worthing (Jolly Brewer) and Upper Beeding (Bridge), to the south; and to the west in Midhurst (Wheatsheaf, Rother) and nearby (Three Moles at Selham, Halfway Bridge in Cowdray Park and Horseguards at Tillington). Between these places and Horsham the red sign is easy to find.

BEERS

Draught   Bitter. A very well hopped and fully flavoured beer.

	Mild. A dark medium-sweet mild.

Mild. A dark medium-sweet mild.

Old. A strong dark beer for the winter.

Bottled   Pale Ale. With some of the bitter's flavour.

Festive. A strong pale ale.

Golding Ale. A barley wine with the smack of hops.

Brown Ale. Medium sweet.

Sussex Wealdman. A strong brown.

J.K. Sweet Stout.

Draught beers are quite heavily dry hopped and drawn from wooden or sometimes metal casks, direct or via manual bar pumps. Some pubs now use a top pressure system.

50   J.W. LEES & CO (BREWERS) LTD

'John Willie Lees'

ADDRESS

Greengate Brewery, Middleton Junction, Manchester, Lancs. Tel 061-643-2487.

Middleton is a Lancashire cotton town about 7 miles north of Manchester. It is one of the oldest towns in the area and a company of Middleton archers fought at the battle of Crécy. In modern times a sophisticated industry makes use of the local skilled labour.

RECOGNITION

Usually 'A Lees House' in green letters is written on the wall of the pub and, in the majority of cases, there is an illuminated sign on which there is a green gate.

TIED HOUSES

These cover an extensive area in the counties of Lancashire and Cheshire and can also be found in North Wales. The greatest concentration is in the Middleton, Oldham, Rochdale area, with the majority of houses being within fifteen miles of the brewery. There are about 35 Lees houses in North Wales, mainly along the coast, as far west as Holyhead in Anglesey and as far south as Corwen near Wrexham. There are nearly 200 houses in all, and the brewery supplies a growing number of clubs.

An extensive pub improvement programme is well under way, which has created pubs with modern amenities but retaining an attractive traditional charm, through a personal approach typical of an independent family brewery.

BEERS

Draught	Bitter. A well-balanced beer. According to a recent survey, it is the strongest of eleven draught bitters tested from the North-West.
	Best Mild. A medium sweet dark mild.
	Mild. A light-coloured mild.
Keg	Bitter. A strong keg bitter with some character.
	Best Mild. Dark in colour.
	Lees Lager. A 'draught' lager which is popular locally.
Bottled	Light Ale.
	Export Ale. A strong pale ale, brewed at export gravity, and sold only in Wales.
	Strong Ale. A high-gravity barley wine.
	Brown Ale. Medium sweet.

Archer Stout. A sweet stout named after the Middleton Archers.

Tulip Lager. A bottled version of Lees Draught Lager.

Edelbrau. A high-gravity lager brewed specially for so-called 'bier kellers'.

In certain traditionally styled houses manual bar pumps are still in use, and in one house draught beer is served direct from the wood. In the busy houses draught beers are dispensed through pillar taps, using either a free-flow system or a pre-measured system sited in the cellar. By adjusting dispensers the beer can be given as much or as little head as the customer requires.

51   MACLAY & CO LTD

'Maclay's Alloa Ales'

ADDRESS

Thistle Brewery, Alloa, Clackmannanshire, Scotland. Tel Alloa 3387/8.

Alloa is the largest town in Clackmannanshire which is the smallest county in Scotland—55 square miles. It is noted for the manufacture of beer, whisky, glass and yarn and has a small harbour on the Forth. Maclay is the only independent brewery north of the Forth.

RECOGNITION

Maclay houses can be recognised by white barrel-shaped illuminated signs depicting the green thistle house sign. 'Maclay's Ales' is written in red and the name of the pub in black. There is not always a sign outside town pubs.

TIED HOUSES

There are 34 of these, mainly in the counties of Clackmannanshire, Ayrshire and Lanarkshire. Wholly owned managed houses are spread over quite a wide area as follows.

In or near Alloa. In Alloa itself (Thistle Bar) and at Alva (Cross Keys), Menstrie (Hollytree Hotel), Clackmannan (Country Hotel) and Stirling (Halfway House).

North of the Forth. At Kincardine (Bridge Bar), Dunfermline (Cartwheel), Inverkeithing (Volunteer Arms) and Aberdour (Foresters Arms).

South of the Forth. At Bridgend near Linlithgow (New Inn) and Loanhead south of Edinburgh (County Bar).

Between Edinburgh and Glasgow. At Forth north of Lanark (Talisker Hotel).

East of Glasgow. At Coatbridge (Forge Inn, The Woodside), Airdrie (Claymore, Commonside Inn, Temple Bar), Uddingston (Rowan Tree) and Hamilton (George Bar).

West of Glasgow. At Johnstone (Stand Bar).

Near the Ayrshire Coast. At Kilwinning (Victoria Bar) and Saltcoats (St Andrews Bar).

Inland in Ayrshire. At Cumnock (Thistle Inn), Dalmellington (Snug Bar), Muirkirk (Central Bar) and Ochiltree (Commercial Inn).

North-east of Dundee. At Arbroath (St Thomas Bar).

Maclay houses are also at Kinross between Perth and Edinburgh and at Comrie to the north-west of Dunfermline. Other pubs in Alloa also sell Maclay's beers.

There is a flourishing free trade.

BEERS

Draught	Maclay's Export.
	Maclay's SPA.
	Maclay's Pale Ale.
	These three well hopped draught bitters are in descending order of strength. Not in all houses.
Keg	Maclay's Keg Export.
	Maclay's Keg Heavy.
	Maclay's Keg Light.
	These three keg beers are also in descending order of strength.
Bottled	India Pale Ale.
	Export. A stronger pale ale.
	Strong Ale. The strongest pale ale.
	Stout. Medium sweet.

Draught beers are dispensed by CO_2, compressed air or direct from cask.

52   McMULLEN & SONS LTD

'Mac's good beer—great pubs'

ADDRESS

26, Old Cross, Hertford, Hertfordshire. Tel 4511.

McMullen & Sons was founded in 1827 and is now the only independent brewery left in the county (although Rayment & Co (33c) still brew).

RECOGNITION

'McMullen' is written on the sign or pub's wall. Occasionally 'Mac's' or 'McMullen's Ales and Stout'. The slogan 'Mac's good beer—great pubs' can be seen on dray lorries, buses etc. Signs are often dark red.

TIED HOUSES

There are nearly 200 Mac's houses which extend into the surrounding counties of Essex, Middlesex and Bedfordshire within thirty miles from Hertford. The majority of houses are within an area bounded by an imaginary line on the map passing through Woodford, west to Boreham Wood, then north through St Albans and Redbourn to Hitchin in north-west Herts. The line turns east to Buntingford and Bishops Stortford, south to Ongar and back to Woodford. Outside this line there are Mac houses at Royston to the north, Hemel Hempstead (Old Town) to the west and in London at Hargrave Place, St Pancras, N7.

An increasing number provide catering facilities.

An extensive free trade is in the above area and also in Watford and North and East London.

BEERS

Draught   Country Best Bitter. A well-balanced and

quite hoppy beer.

AK Best Mild. A light mild very similar to the bitter.

Keg   Castle Keg Special Bitter.

Bottled   Mac's No 1 Pale Ale.

Castle Special Pale Ale. Stronger than Mac's No 1.

Olde Time Ale. A strong ale.

Draught beers are dispensed by top pressure or sometimes by manual bar pumps.

A draught bitter called 'Trad Bitter' is available in 2 gallon and 4½ gallon plastic non-returnable containers with a tap for dispensing. It is similar to the draught bitter but adapted for take-home purposes.

53   MANSFIELD BREWERY CO LTD

'Make mine Mansfield'

ADDRESS

Littleworth, Mansfield, Notts. Tel 25691.

Mansfield is a flourishing town on the river Maun with hosiery mills and nearby coal mining industry. It is a centre for visiting Sherwood Forest.

RECOGNITION

The house sign is a yellow barrel-end and the letter M in green. 'Mansfield' may be written on the sign, or there may be a white illuminated sign with a yellow barrel on which is the pub's name. An older pattern has 'Mansfield' or 'Mansfield Ales' Written on the pub's wall.

TIED HOUSES

There are about 180 licensed houses in Mansfield and surroundings and to the north-west of here at Chesterfield, and they are easy to find in this area.

There is a very flourishing free trade.

BEERS

Draught	Bitter. A well hopped draught bitter.
	Mild. A dark beer.
	Much of the draught beer is delivered in bulk, especially in the free trade.
Bottled	Pale Ale.
	Strong Ale. A strong pale ale.
	Brown Ale.

Draught beer is dispensed by electric pumps and metered dispensers. A few pubs have manual bar pumps.

54   MARSTON, THOMPSON & EVERSHED LTD

'Marston's Burton Ales'

ADDRESS

The Brewery, Shobnall Rd, Burton-upon-Trent, Staffs. Tel 5671.

Burton is the famous brewing town near the centre of England and just to the south-west of Derby, where the history of brewing goes back centuries and was started by the monks. Burton became commercially famous early in the nineteenth century and in 1869 there were 26 breweries in the town. Now there are only 4, of which Marston is one. The hard Burton water was especially suitable for well hopped beers of the pale ale, bitter type.

RECOGNITION

A hanging sign with the pub's name in red and 'Marstons' in black. Colours in use are generally red and black. 'Marston's Burton Ales' may be written on the wall or there may be an illuminated sign with 'Marston's' in red.

TIED HOUSES

There are some 800 of these which are spread over a very wide area in England and Wales as follows.

In Cheshire. Mainly in the Macclesfield/Knutsford area.

In Cumberland. At Raughton Head a few miles south of Carlisle.

In Derbyshire. In an area around Derby bounded by Ashbourne, Buxton, Belper, Shardlow and Repton.

In Hampshire. Mainly in the Winchester/Southampton area and west to Stockbridge and Andover.

In Herefordshire. At Kingstone, Kington and Almely, all quite near Hereford.

In Lancashire. A local concentration in Manchester and surroundings.

In Leicestershire. In Leicester and surroundings as far as Ashby-de-la-Zouch and Loughborough to the north, and Market Harborough to the south.

In Northamptonshire. In the Kettering, Rushden and Corby areas.

In Nottinghamshire. In the Newark area and near Nottingham.

In Shropshire. In the districts of Market Drayton and Wellington.

In Staffordshire. In Burton itself, to the west and south-west of Burton, and around Stoke-on-Trent.

In Warwickshire. In Coventry and nearby.

In Westmorland. At Appleby, Hoff, Morland and Kirkby Stephen.

In Worcestershire. In Worcester and surroundings.

In Caernarvonshire. Spread along the coast at Caernarvon, Croeslon, Talysarn, Penmaenmawr and Llandudno, and inland at Penmachno near Betws-y-Coed.

In Denbighshire. At Ruthin, Clawdd Newydd, Glan Conway, Cerrig-y-Drudion and near the coast at Pensarn and Bodelwyddan.

In Flintshire. Near the coast at Meliden and Gwespyr.

In Merionethshire. At Cynwyd.

There is a free trade spreading beyond the above areas and including London (Cheshire Cheese in Fleet St).

BEERS

Draught	Draught BB (Burton Bitter). Quite a well hopped draught bitter.
	Pedigree. The 'Best Bitter' and perhaps a little sweeter.
	Mild. A dark, medium sweet mild beer.
Keg	Burton Keg. A keg bitter.
	Keg Mild. The draught mild in keg.
Bottled	Light Ale.
	Pedigree. 'Best Burton Pale Ale'. Stronger

than the light ale.

Low Cal. A low-calorie, high-gravity beer.

Owd Roger. A barley wine which is also on draught, but only at the Royal Standard of England, a free house near Forty Green to the north-west of Beaconsfield in Bucks. This is where the brew originated many years ago when it was a home-brewed house.

Nut Brown Ale. A medium sweet brown ale.

Mello Stout. A sweet stout.

Draught beers are dispensed by a top pressure system or by manual bar pumps.

55   MELBOURNS BREWERY LTD

'Stamford Ales'

ADDRESS

All Saints Brewery, Stamford, Lincs. Tel 2200 or 3631.

Stamford is an attractive grey stone town standing on the river Welland just off the A1 and 14 miles north-west of Peterborough.

RECOGNITION

'Melbourns Stamford Ales' written on wall or pub signs, which are all pictorial. The inns are mainly traditional village inns and are decorated individually to blend with the local architecture.

TIED HOUSES

There are just over 30 of these in an area that stretches from Gainsborough in the north to Corby in the south, and Melbourns Stamford Ales can be found going from north to south as follows.

In the Gainsborough area. In the villages of Ingham, Stow and Marton.

In the Lincoln area. In Lincoln itself (eg Waggon & Horses in Burton Rd) and further south at Navenby, Sleaford (Waggon & Horses in Eastgate) and Heckington.

In the Bourne area. At Bourne and in the nearby villages of Rippingale, Haconby, Morton, Dyke, Witham-on-the Hill, Edenham and Grimsthorpe.

In the Stamford area. 4 in Stamford (Hit or Miss, Victoria, Bull & Swan, Jolly Brewer) and in the villages of Ryhall, Great Casterton (2), Tinwell, Easton-on-the-Hill (Blue Bell), South Luffenham, Wakerley and Morcott.

In the Oakham area. In Oakham (Wheatsheaf in Northgate St), Greetham and Wing.

In the Corby area. At Weldon, Deene and Wood-newton.

BEERS

Draught	Bitter. A well flavoured and well hopped brew—from the wood.
	Mild. Dark, medium-sweet and full-bodied. Also from the wood.
Keg	Melbourn Keg. The bitter, matured, chilled and filtered.
	Melbourn Keg Brown. A medium sweet

	mild specially brewed to be chilled and filtered.

Bottled   IPA. A pale ale.

Doublet. An 'export' quality (ie strong) pale ale introduced in spring 1972.

Dinner Ale. A brown ale similar in flavour and quality to the draught mild.

Nut Brown Ale. A stronger brown ale.

Double Stout. A sweet dark stout.

Draught beers are predominantly cellared in wooden casks and dispensed by traditional manual bar pumps, keg beers by top pressure.

56 MITCHELLS OF LANCASTER (BREWERS) LTD

ADDRESS

11, Moor Lane, Lancaster, Lancs. Tel 3773.

Lancaster is the county town of Lancashire on the banks of the river Lune and it is just inland from the seaside resort of Morecambe. There are many old buildings including a castle which stands above the river and is occupied by the law courts. It is open on weekdays from Easter to October. There are many period houses, including an Elizabethan manor built in 1558.

RECOGNITION

The name 'Mitchells' is written outside the pub, either in some position on a wall, or on an illuminated sign which may also have the Red Rose of Lancashire. The trade mark is Lancaster Castle and a drinking 'gentleman' with a long pointed moustache.

TIED HOUSES

There are 47 of these, all within about ten miles of Lancaster. Mitchells houses can easily be found in Lancaster itself, in Morecambe, just south at Galgate and at High and Low Bentham where there are three altogether. These three are in Yorkshire, a few miles to the east of Lancaster and the M6, and just to the north of the Lancashire Fells.

There is a free trade in clubs within the above area.

BEERS

Draught	Bitter. A malty flavoured brew.
	Extra Special Bitter. This is more hopped and much stronger (OG of 1045).
	Mild. A dark mild.
Keg	Keg Bitter. The keg version of the Extra Special Bitter.
	Premium Keg Mild.
Bottled	City Pale Ale.
	City Brown Ale. Medium sweet.
	City Shield Stout. Of high gravity (OG 1045).

Draught beers are dispensed from wooden or metal casks by means of manual bar pumps or electric pumps and counter meters.

57   MORLAND & CO LTD

ADDRESS

The Brewery, Abingdon, Berks. Tel 770.

Abingdon is an old market town just south of Oxford which sprang up around a seventh-century Benedictine abbey part of which is still standing.

Morland's history of brewing in Abingdon goes back to 1711. The company's wine and spirit trade is carried on by Ferguson's Ltd and soft drinks are also produced by the company at Abingdon.

RECOGNITION

The trade mark depicts a painter of the eighteenth century in a red cloak and is connected with a famous artist of that period who was thought to be a member of the Morland family. The painter can be seen on a pale blue plaque outside all Morland pubs and also on an indigo-coloured board which displays the pub's name and 'Morlands' in white letters. Colourful pictorial signs hang outside most Morland houses, and 'Morland' is written in white letters on an indigo-blue background below the sign.

TIED HOUSES

There are around 240 of these spread throughout the counties of Berkshire and south Oxfordshire and overflowing into Hampshire and Surrey. Morland houses may easily be found in many towns and villages in an area on and within an imaginary line passing through Wootton (north of Oxford), then in a clockwise direction through Thame, Windsor, Frimley Green (near Camberley), Hook, Newbury, Hungerford, Faringdon, Brize Norton and back to Wootton.

There is a flourishing free trade.

BEERS

Draught	Bitter. A well hopped draught beer.
	Best Bitter. A full-flavoured stronger beer which is not in all pubs.
	Mild Ale. A medium-dark mild (sometimes called just 'Ale') with an agreeable dryish flavour.
Keg	Keg beers are Whitbread Tankard and Heineken Lager.
Bottled	Morland Light Ale.
	Viking Pale Ale.
	Monarch. A barley wine.
	Brown Ale. Medium sweet.
	Stout. Medium sweet.

Draught beers are mostly dispensed by top pressure CO_2, but in some pubs manual bar pumps remain.

58   MORRELL'S BREWERY LTD

'The beer with the strength of a lion'

ADDRESS

The Lion Brewery, St Thomas Street, Oxford. Tel 42013.

RECOGNITION

The house or trade mark is a blue and white plaque with a golden lion rampant on a white tankard. Signs and pub walls usually have 'Morrell's' and 'Morrell's Ales and Stout' written in pale blue letters with white borders.

TIED HOUSES

Morrell's beers can be drunk in 140 pubs in the city of learning itself and within a thirty-mile radius in surrounding towns and villages. Outposts are at Banbury (23 miles north of Oxford), Bicester (a few miles north of Oxford), Thame and Chinnor to the east, and Swindon 29 miles to the south-west. Then southwards at Goring-on-Thames towards Reading. Many towns and villages within this area have Morrell houses.

BEERS

Draught	Bitter. A well-balanced draught beer.
	Light Ale. A lighter version of the bitter.
	College Ale. A stronger ale to be found in some pubs.
Keg	Varsity Keg. A medium-gravity keg beer.
	Pale Ale Keg. Of lighter gravity.
	These are chilled and filtered but not pasteurised.
Bottled	Light Oxford Ale.
	Castle Ale. A medium-gravity pale ale.
	College Ale. A barley wine.
	Brown Ale.
	Malt Stout.

Draught beers are dispensed by manual bar pumps or direct from the cask (in a few pubs), but top pressure is also used, especially where the cellar is not too deep and the risk of the beer becoming too gassy is minimised.

59   THE NORTHERN CLUBS' FEDERATION BREWERY LTD

ADDRESS

Forth Street, Newcastle-upon-Tyne, Northumberland. Tel 610591-7.

SOME HISTORY AND FACTS OF INTEREST

The Clubs' Brewery was initiated at a meeting of club committees at Prudhoe-on-Tyne in 1919, as a result of the shortage of beer supplies to the clubs after the war. The first brew of Federation Ale was produced in March 1921, since when the brewery has expanded steadily and all beers are now produced and retailed by cellar tank, keg and bottle. All beers leaving the brewery are naturally conditioned and filtered ready for immediate sale.

The company is run as a co-operative venture, the shareholders being the clubs who sell the beers. These shareholding clubs receive dividends for their purchases and the total amount paid out since the beginning exceeds £23 million, more than £7 million of this having been paid out in the last five years.

For several years the brewery has been the only one in the country to declare the original gravity of all its beers on bottle labels, advertising etc.

TRADING AREA

Almost 900 clubs sell Federation Ale. The trading area covers the north of England—from Berwick-on-Tweed to north Yorkshire on the east coast, from south-west Scotland to north Lancashire on the west coast, the Coventry area of the Midlands (contact man to be found at Radford Road Social Club), and the St Austell area of Cornwall. Clubs in Yorkshire, Lancashire and the North Midlands also receive Federation Ales via the Yorkshire Clubs' Brewery. There is a hotel near Sunderland which supplies Federation Ales—The Post House Hotel (Trust House-Forte) at Washington.

BEERS

Draught	Federation Pale Ale. OG 1032. Cellar tank and keg.
	Federation Special Ale. OG 1041. Cellar tank and keg.
	Both are well-flavoured beers with a smack of hops. All tank beers are kept in refrigerated cellars and are dispensed via pumps through measured dispensers.
Bottled	'Ace of Clubs' brand names:
	Special Ale. A pale ale of OG 1041.
	Export. A stronger pale ale. OG 1046.
	Light Brown Ale. OG 1032.
	Strong Brown Ale. OG 1047.
	Sweet Stout. OG 1044.

The Clubs' Brewery bottles Guinness and Harp Lager for the clubs. A wide selection of wines and spirits are also offered for sale.

60   OKELL & SON LTD

'The brewers of quality beers'

ADDRESS

Falcon Brewery, Douglas, Isle of Man. Tel 3034/5.

Licensing laws in the Isle of Man have long been more relaxed than on the mainland: in summer, 10 am to 11 pm, and in winter, noon to 10 pm.

RECOGNITION

'Okell's Ales' may be written on the wall of the pub, or there may be a signboard with 'Okell's Ales mild and bitter on draught' with a picture of the Falcon trade mark in a white circle. Alternatively 'Okell's Ales on draught and in bottle' may be seen on the pub wall. Some pubs may have 'Manington's' or 'Heron & Brearley' written on the wall and there are a few with no recognition sign at all.

TIED HOUSES

There are approaching 80 of these and they may be found without difficulty throughout the whole of the island. Manington's have 5 residential hotels—2 in Douglas (Castle Mona, Central) and 3 in Port Erin (Belle Vue, Falcon's Nest, Eagle). Heron & Brearley have the Queens Hotel in Douglas and approximately 15 tenanted houses.

BEERS

Draught	Bitter. A draught beer with a good hopping rate.
	Mild. A dark mild which is not in all pubs.
Keg	Falcon Keg Bitter.
Bottled	Falcon Pale Ale.

Falcon Nut Brown. A medium sweet brown ale.

Falcon No 1 Strong Ale. Barley wine type.

Draught beers are dispensed by means of manual bar pumps, or in some cases by the Tap Pillar system with an electric impeller in which the beer can be dispensed more or less aerated according to requirements by means of a sparklet.

61   OLDHAM BREWERY CO LTD

'Oldham Ales'

ADDRESS

Albion Brewery, Coldhurst Street, Oldham, Lancs. Tel 061-624-8395.

Oldham is an old-established cotton-spinning town on a hill to the north-east of Manchester and it is noted for the manufacture of textile machinery.

RECOGNITION

'Oldham Ales' may be written in red on the wall of the pub, or 'an OB house'. The house sign is 'OB' in white written inside a red bell, and this may be seen on a plaque on the front wall of the pub.

TIED HOUSES

There are around 100 licensed houses, mostly within

5-10 miles of Oldham. There are 3 in Rochdale to the north, 2 in Middleton to the west, 2 in Saddleworth to the east and 1 in Ashton just south of Oldham. There is a free trade within the area.

BEERS

Draught	Bitter. A well hopped draught beer.
	Mild. A full-bodied, medium sweet, dark mild.
Keg	A keg bitter and keg mild have recently been developed.
	Golden Keg. A 'draught' lager.
Bottled	Pale Ale.
	Brown Ale.
	Old Tom. A strong, dark barley wine.
	Oldham Stout. A medium sweet stout.

Draught beers are dispensed mostly by electric pumps and a measured meter, or top pressure, or by manual bar pumps. About 60 per cent of draught beer is supplied in tanks incorporating a pneumatic dispensing system, but it all depends on the pub's cellar and its particular requirements.

62   PAINE & CO LTD

ADDRESS

The Counting House, Market Square, St Neots, Hunts. Tel Huntingdon 72581.

St Neots is just off the A1, 17 miles west of Cambridge and on the A45 which is one of the main routes from the Midlands to the East Coast. The brewery lies just off the market square, which is the second largest in the country.

RECOGNITION

'Paine & Co Ltd' in pale blue letters with a white border is easily identifiable on the pub wall. A few houses have 'Paine & Co' in red, but these are being replaced.

TIED HOUSES

Seven of the 24 'Paine' houses are at St Neots itself and another is at each of the adjoining villages of Eynesbury and Eaton Socon. To the south Paine's Ales may be enjoyed at Girtford on the A1 just north of Sandy and at Great Barford on the road to Bedford. Then west of Bedford at Turvey and further north in the villages of Bolnhurst, Great Staughton, Upper Dean, Tilbrook, Kimbolton (New Sun Inn) and Lowick (which is near Thrapston); also at Sawtry (just off the A1). Nearer St Neots, look for the Paine signs at Huntingdon (Victoria Inn), Brampton (Brampton Hotel on the A1), Little Paxton, Abbotsley and Caxton Gibbet (on the Cambridge road). There is a little free trade in and around St Neots.

BEERS

Draught	XXX Bitter. A light bitter with a pleasing malty flavour.
	Special Mild. A dark beer.
Bottled	Pale Ale.
	Extra Ale. Strong and well hopped.
	Gold Medal Ale. The bitter in bottle, but a little sweeter and stronger.
	Brown Ale. Medium sweet.

Draught beers are dispensed by top pressure.

63   J.C. & R.H. PALMER

'Palmer's Ales'

ADDRESS

Old Brewery, West Bay Road, Bridport, Dorset. Tel 2396/7.

Bridport is a small West Dorset town 15 miles west of Dorchester and 1½ miles north of the harbour and holiday beach of West Bay. It is noted for the manufacture of ropes, twines and fishing nets. The brewery is set in semi-rural surroundings on the road to West Bay and is unique in being the only brewery in the country with a thatched roof.

RECOGNITION

Colourful pictorial signs, generally with a basic background colour of pale blue, can be seen outside Palmer's pubs. There is also a small illuminated sign depicting 'Palmer's Ales' in red (Palmer's) and blue (Ales) letters.

TIED HOUSES

There are 60-70 of these which are easy to find in Bridport and many of the surrounding towns and villages. Outposts are at Lyme Regis, Axminster (Devon), Crewkerne (Somerset) and Maiden Newton (north-west of Dorchester). A guide to some of the pubs can be obtained at the brewery.

BEERS

Draught	BB. A well-balanced draught beer with a certain malty flavour.
	IPA. A stronger version of the BB.
Bottled	Light Pale Ale.
	IPA. A stronger light ale.
	Tally Ho Strong Ale. Stronger than the IPA.
	Nut Brown Ale. Medium sweet.
	Extra Stout. Medium sweet.

Draught beers are supplied in stainless steel casks (except for pins which are in aluminium casks) and mostly under top pressure. There are a few houses with manual bar pumps or dispensing direct from casks. No keg beers are produced, as the draught beers satisfy the local demand.

64   RANDALLS BREWERY LTD

'Randalls beers are part of the Island'
'Boxer Ales always win on points'

ADDRESS

Clare Street, St Helier, Jersey, Channel Islands.

Jersey is the largest and most southerly of the Channel Isles and it has one of the highest sunshine records in the British Isles—just over 1,900 hours annually compared with around 1,600 for London and around 1,800 on the South Coast. It is only 14 miles from France.

The pubs on Jersey are open all day until 11 pm in the evening, and beer is cheaper than in the UK.

RECOGNITION

'Randalls Boxer Beers' may be written on the pub wall, or sometimes 'Randalls Beers' or 'Boxer Ales'.

TIED HOUSES

There are 29 or so ties, out of which 8 or 9 are shared with wine merchants. The bulk of the trade is free, and Boxer Beers may be drunk all over the island. Out of about 500 licences in Jersey less than 100 are tied.

BEERS

Keg	Randalls Island Draught Beer. This is a naturally conditioned keg bitter with above average hopping rate. It has true traditional draught characteristics as opposed to keg and there is no pasteurisation process.
	Grunhalle Lager. This lager was conceived at Randalls and as a result of its success a separate company was formed called Grunhalle International which franchises it to other brewers.
Bottled	Boxer Pale Ale. Is matured for a month and has a high hop rate.
	Boxer Brown Ale. A characteristic sweetish flavour.
	Grunhalle Lager. The 'draught' lager in bottle.

The brewery bottles Brewmaster. Harp Lager, Heineken Lager, John Courage and Tuborg Lager. Whitbread Tankard is available in the pubs.

Keg beers are dispensed by top pressure.

65   R.W. RANDALL LTD

'Bobby Ales'
'VB Ales and Stout'

ADDRESS

Vauxlaurens Brewery, St Julians Avenue, St Peter Port, Guernsey, Channel Islands. Tel 20134.

There is a deep well at the brewery with a supply of pure water from which all the beer is brewed.

Licensing laws are less strict than in the United Kingdom and pubs are open from 10.30 am until 11 pm. Some have a short break between 2 pm and 4.30 or 5 pm, except in St Peter Port, where the majority stay open throughout the licensing hours.

Beers in Guernsey average at about an OG of 1042 compared with 1037 in the UK. They are also cheaper.

RECOGNITION

As is the custom in Guernsey, there is no brewer's distinguishing sign on tied premises. The trade mark is VB after the name of the brewery.

TIED HOUSES

There are 17 of these but most of the trade is free and 'Bobby Ales' can be found all over the island and also in Alderney and Sark. A number of the tied houses are jointly owned by wine merchants, which is a common practice in the Channel Isles.

BEERS

Draught	XX Mild. A medium dark and well hopped mild ale.
Keg	Bobby Keg Bitter. A keg beer of high gravity.
Bottled	Bobby IPA Red Top. A light ale similar to the keg but with more hops.
	Bobby Ale. The XX Mild in bottle.
	Stout. Medium sweet.

Bottled Guinness and other beers are available and also Breda Lager from Belgium in bottle and draught. Keg dispensed by top pressure and draught by manual bar pumps.

66   T.D. RIDLEY & SONS LTD

'Draught Beer from the Wood'

ADDRESS

Orchard House, Mill Road, Chelmsford, Essex. Tel 53513.

Chelmsford is the county town of Essex and is 32 miles north-east of London. The brewery is at the village of Hartford End (tel Great Dunmow 820316) which is eight miles north of the Chelmsford-Great Dunmow road and about half-way between the two towns. It was here that the firm was founded in the early 1840s and it had its beginning in a small water mill. From this developed a flour milling business in Chelmsford—later closed—two maltings, also in Chelmsford, and the brewery at Hartford End, where conditions are particularly suited to beer production.

RECOGNITION

'Ridleys' is written in gold outside the pubs on a green or blue background and is quite conspicuous. The symbol 'Draught Beer from the Wood' is used on internal utensils such as bar towels and drip mats.

TIED HOUSES

There are just over 60 of these in many towns and villages of central and north-west Essex. The majority lie within an area defined by the road from Chelmsford (where there are 6—Bird in Hand, Globe, New Barn, Red Lion, Ship, Woolpack) going north-west to White Roding; then north-east through Great Dunmow to Finchingfield; then south-east to Blackmore End, Stisted, Braintree and back to Chelmsford. Outside this area there are Ridley houses as follows.

At and near Saffron Walden At Saffron Walden (The Sun) and Great Sampford to the east.

In and around Great Dunmow. At Duton Hill, Little Easton, Canfield and Takeley. Also on the road north out of Dunmow (Cricketers).

To the east of Chelmsford. At Fairstead, Ranks Green, White Notley, Messing, Little Braxted, Witham (George, Swan, Victoria), Wickham Bishops, Hatfield Peverel, Boreham and Cock Clarks.

South of Chelmsford. At Great Baddow, Rettendon, Margaretting and Mountnessing.

West of Chelmsford. At Radley Green, Boards Green and Mashbury.

BEERS

Draught   Bitter. Well hopped with a good flavour. Mild. A dark draught mild.

Keg	Bitter. Well flavoured for a keg beer, also well hopped.
Bottled	Essex Ale. A light ale.
	Old Bob. A strong pale ale.
	Stock. A strong dark ale.
	Bishop Ale. A barley wine.
	Brown Ale.
	Stout.

All draught beers are from wooden casks and are dispensed direct or by manual bar pumps or electric pumps.

67   FREDERIC ROBINSON LTD

'Robinsons'

ADDRESS

Unicorn Brewery, Stockport, Cheshire. Tel 6571.

Stockport is a cotton-spinning and hat-making town which lies on the slopes of the Mersey Valley a few miles to the south-east of Manchester.

RECOGNITION

Look out for the Unicorn house sign which is situated on the pub's wall on a pale blue plaque. Also written on the pub's wall may be the name 'Robinsons' and the name of the house. There may be a pictorial sign with 'Robinsons' written in an illuminated canopy above the painting.

TIED HOUSES

There are approximately 300 of these, the majority

of which are in the north-east Cheshire area and extending over the whole of Manchester and its close suburbs and well into Cheshire, Derbyshire and North Wales. The main trading area falls along and within an imaginary line from Bakewell in Derbyshire clockwise to Nantwich (Horse Shoe on the A52, Rifleman in James Hall St), up to Tarporley (Rising Sun), Cotebrook, Whitegate, Tabley, Little Hulton (south of Bolton), Whitefield, Rochdale (Healey Hotel, St James Tavern), Uppermill, Glossop, Castleton and back to Bakewell. Outside this area there are Robinson houses at Whittington near Oswestry, to the north at Garstang (Royal Oak) between Preston and Lancaster, nearby at Catforth, Balderstone and Preston itself (Black Horse in Friargate).

Robinson houses in North Wales include the following. Anglesey: Beaumaris, Glyngarth, Menai Bridge, Moelfre, Dulas and Bull Bay. Caernarvonshire: Beddgelert, Garn Dolbenmaen, Nantperis. Merionethshire: Dolgellau, Llanbedr. Denbighshire: Llanfair Talhaiarn, Llangollen, Llansannan, Ruabon, Ruthin.

A guide to the pubs and hotels called 'Sightseeing with the Unicorn' has been published for the brewery.

BEERS

Draught	Best Bitter. Quite a well hopped draught beer.
	Best Mild. A light mild.
Keg	Cock Robin Keg Bitter.
	Einhorn Draught Lager.
Bottled	Light Ale.
& cans	Pale Ale. Stronger.
	Party Brew. A bitter ale in 4 pint cans.

Old Tom. A barley wine.
Brown Ale.
Unicorn Stout. Medium sweet.

Draught beers are dispensed by top pressure, electric pumps and meters or manual bar pumps.

68   G. RUDDLE & CO LTD

'Ruddles Fine Ales'

ADDRESS

The Brewery, Langham, Oakham, Rutland. Tel Oakham 2512/3.

There is a castle at Oakham which is in the centre of rolling fox-hunting country.

RECOGNITION

White circular signs on a blue background with 'Ruddles' written in the upper portion of the circle and the name of the pub in the bottom portion and a pictorial sign in the centre. These are gradually replacing the rectangular pictorial signs with the pub's name and 'Ruddles' written on a blue strip above and below the picture.

TIED HOUSES

Forty-four of these, situated for the most part in pleasant rolling countryside. Many do bed and breakfast and all provide food of some sort. Taking Oakham as the centre, Ruddles country extends on an approximate 15-mile radius taking in Melton Mowbray, Peterborough, Market Deeping and

Stamford. Approaching from outside, the first Ruddles houses that may be encountered are, from the south, on the Kettering-Uppingham road near Corby (Knights Lodge), then in a clockwise direction at Hallaton to the north-east of Market Harborough; Illston-on-the-Hill; Billesdon, just off the A47 east of Leicester; Gaddesby; Melton Mowbray (Noel Arms); Redmile west of Grantham and Marston to the north; to the south-east at Old Somerby, Irnham, Morton and Little Bytham; Market Deeping (The Bull) and Barnack; and the most south-eastern approaches are through Peterborough (Elephant & Castle) and St Neots (Greenacres). Ruddles territory may also be entered near Oundle at Southwick or Stoke Doyle where there are Ruddles houses. There are several in Stamford and one just off the A1 at Stretton. Once within this outer circle the pubs are easily found.

A map giving information about the pubs can be obtained from the brewery or the pubs themselves.

There is a free trade which extends slightly further than the above area and includes Nottingham, Leicester, Kettering and Market Harborough.

BEERS

Draught	Bitter. An agreeable draught beer.
	County. Exceptionally strong and well hopped.
	Barley Wine. A new beer produced for the present on festive occasions such as Christmas.
Container beers	Classic. A container beer version of the draught County.
	Keg. A special brew, stronger and hoppier than many keg beers.

Bitter. A container beer version of the draught bitter.

Mild. Dark and full bodied.

Langdorf. A lager brewed at Langham.

Bottled   Light Ale. Also in non-returnable bottles (NRB).

Export NRB.

County.

These two are stronger light ales.

Rutland Ale. Barley wine.

Bob Brown. A brown ale also in NRB.

Ruddles Strong Brown. A new beer brewed at 1048 and full-bodied.

Draught beers are dispensed by manual bar pumps, or in a few cases direct from the cask. Container beers by CO_2 on a free-flow system.

69   ST AUSTELL BREWERY CO LTD

'St Austell Ales'

ADDRESS

St Austell, Cornwall. Tel 2444.

St Austell is a mid-Cornish town, not far from the South Coast, which is famous for its china clay mines.

RECOGNITION

No mistaking the black inn-signs pointing the way to 'St Austell Ales' in gold letters.

TIED HOUSES

Most of the 135 pubs are concentrated in south-west

Cornwall, roughly west of a line from north to south passing through Delabole, Camelford and Fowey in all of which there are St Austell houses. East of this line there are outposts at Bude (The Globe), Crow's Nest north of Liskeard (Sun Inn), at Liskeard (Barley Sheaf), Hessenford (Copley Arms) and Looe (The Ship). West of here St Austell pubs are plentiful and easy to find. The south-western outpost is in the Scillies at St Mary's (the Bishop & Wolf Inn). No less than 74 are inns or hotels offering accommodation— 25 on or near the north coast, 17 inland and 32 on or near the south coast.

A map of Cornwall naming the pubs is displayed in many of the houses, and this, or a tea towel with a similar map, can be obtained from the brewery.

There is a substantial free trade.

BEERS

Draught	BB. A draught bitter with a good malty flavour.
	St Austell XXXX. A dark mild.
Keg	St Austell Extra. A keg bitter that was introduced as long ago as the early fifties. Filtered but not pasteurised.
Bottled	Light Ale.
	Brown Ale.
	Duchy Special Pale Ale. A stronger PA with a good hop flavour.
	Smuggler's Ale. A strong ale.
	Prince's Ale. A barley wine which was intended as 'a once only, strength no object' brew to commemorate Prince Charles' 21st birthday. It is one of the

strongest beers brewed and proved so popular that it is brewed regularly with sales increasing.

Draught beers are dispensed by manual bar pumps, direct from wooden casks or by top pressure, the keg beer by top pressure.

70   SELBY (MIDDLEBROUGH) BREWERY LTD

ADDRESS

The Brewery, Millgate, Selby, Yorkshire. Tel 2826.

This is an old-established company that ceased brewing in 1954 and since that date has been engaged in the bottling of Guinness and the distribution of a variety of beers and soft drinks to many clubs and free houses in Selby and much of the surrounding area. In one respect, it is unique in the brewing industry: unlike the large number of companies that have ceased brewing in recent years, it has reversed the trend and has recommenced brewing operations. Thanks to the enthusiasm of the present owner, who descends from the owners when brewing ceased in 1954, the old brewery with new equipment sprang back to life in December 1972. In that month the first brew for nearly twenty years was made—with loving care—and passed out of the brewery to some of the free trading pubs and clubs in Selby and the surrounding area.

The Selby brew is a strong draught bitter with a characteristic and agreeable flavour. It is dispensed from specially made wooden casks and is a real draught beer brewed in the traditional manner and only from malt and hops—no additional sugar is used.

Later on, it is possible that other beers will be brewed.

Outlets for the beer may be as far apart as clubs in Newcastle-upon-Tyne and Sheffield. Some of the free pubs in the Selby and York area will probably sell it—such as in Thorganby and Ellerton south of York and Cawood north of Selby and other places. The nearest source can be quickly discovered by a call to the brewery.

71   SHEPHERD NEAME LTD

'Master Brewers'

ADDRESS

Faversham Brewery, 17 Court Street, Faversham, Kent. Tel 2206/9.

Faversham has for long been a brewing town, not far from the North Kent coast just south of the Swale—the channel which separates the Isle of Sheppey from the mainland. There are many buildings in the town dating back some centuries and Draught Abbey and Abbey Ale take their names from the abbey built in 1147 by King Stephen of which there are only a few remains.

RECOGNITION

The conspicuous white signs with 'Shepherd Neame Master Brewers' in red and black letters point the way to Shepherd Neame ales, as does also the white plaque on the wall of many pubs. 'Shepherd Neame

Ltd Faversham Ales' is sometimes to be seen and the company trade mark is a shepherd's crook and a letter 'N' which is shaped like an inverted 'U' in red and black. Newly decorated houses have red signboards.

In addition there may be red signs with white lettering indicating the type of food available. 'Abbey Eating House' indicates a full menu during licensing hours; 'Grills' points the way to at least two different joints; and 'Snacks' to a variety of hot snacks.

TIED HOUSES

Well over 200 of these covering a wide area in East Kent; as far as Tenterden and Hawkhurst in the Weald and Hastings (Prince Albert in Cornwallis St) and St Leonard's (Prince of Wales, Western Road) on the coast; just inland at Battle (Abbey Hotel); Tunbridge Wells (Imperial Hotel, Southborough; Royal Oak in Speldhurst Rd); Tonbridge (Foresters Arms in Quarry Hill); a village—Rusthall—west of Tunbridge Wells (White Hart); and Brasted on the A25 near Westerham. At most points east of these places Shepherd Neame houses can easily be found. In addition there are several in Greater London: near Smithfield Market (Rutland Hotel); at Croydon (Two Brewers); at Forest Hill (Railway Telegraph); in Woolwich New Rd (Anglesey Arms); at Bromley (Bricklayers Arms); at Chislehurst Common (Crown); and at Deptford (Harp of Erin).

There is an extensive free trade—one-third of all trade is with clubs as far apart as Shoeburyness, St Albans and Frimley Green.

BEERS

Draught	Bitter. Very well hopped and agreeably flavoured.
	Best Bitter. Slightly stronger and in only a few pubs.
	Light Mild. A lightish refreshing drink not unlike the Bitter in hop flavour. Available in most clubs and in the tied trade only in the Isle of Sheppey.
	Mild. A dark beer.
	Old English Stock Ale. A strong 'Old' ale brewed all the year round but not in many pubs in the summer.
Keg	Draught Abbey. A keg bitter with a smooth, characteristic flavour. In many free houses.
	Hurlimann Swiss Lager. Shepherd Neame are the sole importers.
Bottled	Light Ale.
	Abbey Ale. A medium-strength pale ale.
	Bishop's Finger. A light strong ale.
	Christmas Ale. A very strong beer for the festive season.
	Brown Ale.

Draught beers, from wood or metal casks, are dispensed by manual bar pumps and in a few places by electric pumps or top pressure.

72   JAMES SHIPSTONE & SONS LTD

'Shipstone of Nottingham'

ADDRESS

Star Brewery, New Basford, Nottingham. Tel 75074.

RECOGNITION

Very often 'Shipstone Ales' is written in red on a yellow illuminated sign. Variations on this are 'A Shipstone House' and the pub's name in blue, and the sign may be white. Sometimes 'Shipstone's' or 'Shipstone's Ales' is written on the pub's wall.

TIED HOUSES

Several hundred licensed houses in Nottingham city and county, Leicester city and county, and Derbyshire. Some representation in Lincolnshire (eg Grantham, Horncastle) and Yorkshire. There is an extensive free trade in this area.

BEERS

Draught	Bitter. A well hopped draught beer.
	Mild. A dark mild also well hopped.
Keg	Keg Bitter.
Bottled	India Pale Ale.
	Gold Star Ale. A light gravity pale ale.
	Strong Ale. A strong dark beer.
	Nut Brown Ale.
	Ship Stout. Medium sweet.

Draught beers are dispensed by electric pumps and in some cases manual bar pumps.

73   SAMUEL SMITH OLD BREWERY (TADCASTER) LTD

ADDRESS

The Old Brewery, Tadcaster, Yorks. Tel 2225.

Tadcaster is a famous brewing town on the river Wharfe ten miles south-west of York. Samuel Smith have two operating breweries—one at Tadcaster and a subsidiary at Rochdale in Lancashire, The Rochdale & Manor Brewery Ltd.

RECOGNITION

Black signboards with the pub's name and 'Samuel Smith' written in gold gothic lettering. The white rose of Yorkshire is depicted on a plaque on a wall of the pub and 'Yorkshire's oldest brewery' may be written on a black board. Some pubs may still have the old red signboards advertising 'Taddy Ales', but these are gradually being replaced.

TIED HOUSES

There are nearly 300 of these scattered from Tyneside to Northamptonshire. Some of the outposts can be found as follows: in Lincolnshire at Stamford (Vaults), in Louth (Masons Arms), at Spalding (Old White Horse); and in Northants at Corby (Rockingham Arms). In Lancashire there is a concentration of Samuel Smith houses in the Rochdale, Oldham and Manchester areas; and in Cheshire a few in the Altrincham district.

There is a very flourishing free trade which forms the bulk of the business.

BEERS

Draught   Bitter. A draught bitter with a malty

character.

Light Mild. A lighter version of the bitter.

4X Best Mild. A dark mild beer.

Strong Ale.

Container beers	These are Super Bitter, Super 4X, Super Strong Ale, Special Mild, Sovereign Bitter and Alpine Lager. Sovereign Bitter is a keg bitter and Alpine Lager is brewed under licence from a Bavarian brewery.
Bottled	Taddy Light.

Taddy Bitter. Slightly more bitter than the light.

Sovereign Pale Ale. A strong pale ale.

Old Samson. An old ale.

Taddy Golden Ale. A barley wine.

Taddy Nut Brown Ale. Medium sweet.

Alpine Lager. The 'draught' lager in bottle.

Taddy Bitter Ale, Taddy Nut Brown, Alpine Lager and Sovereign Pale Ale are also in one-trip bottles.

Draught beers are dispensed by a bar metering system with an electric pump or in some cases by manual bar pumps.

74   SOUTH WALES AND MONMOUTHSHIRE UNITED CLUBS BREWERY CO LTD

ADDRESS

Crown Brewery, Pontyclun, Glamorganshire. Tel Pontyclun 453/4/5.

Pontyclun, 10 miles north-west of Cardiff, is a

small town close by Llantrisant where the national coinage is minted.

SOME HISTORY AND FACTS OF INTEREST

The difficulty that clubs and institutes had in obtaining supplies of beer towards the end of World War I led to the formation of the United Clubs Brewery in July 1919 and an option was obtained on a brewery at Pontyclun. It was in March 1919 at the Cathays Liberal Club in Cardiff, at a representative meeting of the South Wales Branch Clubs, that a resolution was carried giving birth to the undertaking. The necessary finance was raised by the issue of share capital which is now entirely in the hands of the clubs and its members. Trade expanded and in 1954 a new brewery was completed. It is interesting to note that the financing of this new brewery was given considerable help by the Northern Clubs' Federation Brewery (no 59) of Newcastle by means of a low-interest loan. The company has adopted the co-operative principles of trading and from 1920 to the present day well over £3 million has been returned to clubs from their trading with the company.

TRADING AREA

The Clubs Brewery supplies 350-360 free trading clubs over a wide area from Coleford (near Monmouth) in the east, along the South Wales coast as far as Carmarthen and to Brecon further north. The trading area is continually expanding and United Clubs Brewery beers are also supplied to clubs in the Birmingham and Chippenham (Wilts) areas.

BEERS

Draught	CPA (Clubs Pale Ale).
	SBB (Special Bitter Beer). Stronger than the CPA.

> Both are true draught beers in cask with a pronounced hoppy flavour. Bitter in tank. This is the CPA or SBB chilled, filtered and carbonated, delivered by tanker and dispensed from tanks at the club.

Keg	Crown Keg Beer. A pasteurised keg bitter of pleasant flavour.
Bottled	Clubs Amber. A light ale.
	Clubs Special. A stronger light ale.
	Clubs Extra. The strongest light ale.
	Clubs Brown Ale. A sweetish brown ale.

Some clubs still use manual bar pumps for dispensing draught beer, but the pumps are rapidly being replaced by electric cellar pumps. In some instances the beer is dispensed by top pressure alone, but all tank beer installations combine top pressure with an electric pump and measured dispensers.

National beers such as Guinness, Harp Lager, Mackeson, Manns Brown Ale and Tuborg Lager are bottled and supplied by the brewery.

75   TIMOTHY TAYLOR & CO LTD

'Taylor's Ales'

ADDRESS

Knowle Spring Brewery, Keighley, Yorks. Tel 3139.
Keighley (pronounced Keethly) is a small manu-

facturing town on the north edge of the Pennines and 18 miles to the west of Leeds.

RECOGNITION

Often a hanging pictorial sign with 'Taylor' or 'Taylor's Ales' written above the picture. The name 'Taylor' may be on a separate sign, often on a green background. A barley sheaf on a white background may also be on the pub's wall.

TIED HOUSES

Not far off 30 of these, many of which are in Keighley itself. Others can be found as follows. On the road to Colne at Glusburn (Dog & Gun); north of here at Cononley (New Inn); at Colne (Hare & Hounds at Black Lane Ends about three miles out past the golf course on the Old Skipton Road); towards Bradford at Bingley (Brown Cow, Ferrands Arms); south of Keighley at Oakworth (Grouse Inn two miles out on the Colne road) and Haworth (Fleece); north of Hebden Bridge at Heptonstall and two more in the surrounding hills (Mount Skip, Hare & Hounds).

There is a free trade.

BEERS

Draught beers include a very well flavoured Best Bitter and light bitter (called Golden Best Light Mild) both with the smack of hops, a stronger bitter called Draught Landlord, a dark mild and old which is a strong dark ale. Bottled beers are Special Pale Ale,

Blue Label and Landlord which are stronger pale ales, a dark ale called Northerner No 1 and a medium sweet stout—Black Bess.

Draught beers are mainly dispensed by electric pumps with a counter metering system or manual bar pumps.

76   T. & R. THEAKSTON LTD

ADDRESS

Wellgarth, Masham, Ripon, Yorks. Tel Masham 206.

Masham is a small North Yorkshire town on the edge of the Dales country and it is noted for the size of its market place. The brewery is in Red Lane.

T. & R. Theakston are family brewers founded in 1827 and still very much independent. All their houses serve true traditional draught beer from the wood, and to preserve this tradition a cooper is employed by the company.

RECOGNITION

'Theakstons' in most cases, but not all, is written on the outside wall of the pub. The trade mark is a black bull which in future years will be used as a guide to Theakston houses.

TIED HOUSES

There are 16 of these and a complete list is given on a drip mat to be found in the pubs. There are 3 in Masham itself (Kings Head, White Bear and Bay

Horse); 2 in Ripon (Black Bull and Magdalens), and
the Busby Stoop on the main crossroads just west of
Thirsk. Here there is a chair with a legend of
unpleasant happenings coming to those who sit on it.
To the north and east of the A1 there is the Fleece at
Northallerton; Black Swan at Brompton; Non-Plus at
Morton-at-Swale; Bay Horse at Catterick; and White
Heifer at Scorton. Towards Middlesbrough there is
the Station at Hutton Rudby. Then west of Catterick
the Holly Hill at Richmond and Clarendon at Marske.
There is one in the heart of the Dale country at
Hawes (Crown) and between there and Masham at
Middleham (Black Swan).

There is also a free trade.

BEERS

Draught	Best Bitter. A very pale, well-balanced draught beer.
	Old Peculiar. A dark 'Strong Yorkshire Ale' of distinctive flavour. Stated to be one of the strongest on draught from the wood.
Bottled	Pale Ale.
	Export. Stronger and darker.
	Old Peculiar. The draught OP in bottle.
	Brown Ale. Medium sweet.

Draught beers are dispensed mainly by manual bar
pumps and in a few cases by electric pumps.

77   DANIEL THWAITES & COMPANY LTD

'Thwaites Ales'

ADDRESS

Star Brewery, Blackburn, Lancs. Tel 54431.
  Shire horses are still used by Thwaites for deliveries in and around the town. The modern brewhouse in the town centre was completed in 1966.

RECOGNITION

Thwaites houses are easily spotted, either in the colours of red and white or in new colours and new-style lettering of black and grey backgrounds with red lettering. All country pubs are in black and white and all pubs have a sign reading either 'Thwaites' or 'Its a Thwaites House', the latter being normally an electric box sign.

TIED HOUSES

There are 380 stretching from Grange-over-Sands in the north (on the coast south of the Lake District) and throughout Lancashire down to Cheshire and the Potteries. In Cheshire, Thwaites Ales may be drunk in Congleton, Knutsford, Glossop and Hayfield; and further south at Market Drayton, Hilderstone (south of Stoke) and Wyaston near Ashbourne.
  Free trade extends from Cumberland to South Staffs and over the West Riding of Yorkshire. In London in Southwark St (The Dive Bar).

BEERS

Draught   Bitter. A full, distinctive flavoured

	draught beer.
	Mild. A darkish mild of Lancashire type.
	Best Mild. A sweeter mild.
Keg	Starkeg. A keg bitter.
	Dannykeg. Keg Best Mild.
Bottled	East Lancs. A pale ale.
	Big Ben. Dark strong ale.
	Old Dan Nips. Extra strong dark ale.
	Green Top. Brown ale.
	Danny Brown. Sweet Brown ale.

Draught beers are dispensed by bar pumps in smaller houses but in larger houses where large quantities of beer are served the Porter Lancastrian system (which uses compressed air for the motive power, assisted by top pressure from the beer container) is coupled with bulk tanks. Otherwise the traditional English cask beer is favoured.

78 TOLLEMACHE & COBBOLD BREWERIES LTD

ADDRESS

Cliff Brewery, Ipswich, Suffolk. Tel 57481.

Ipswich is the county town of East Suffolk and lies at the head of the estuary of the river Orwell. It is a thriving port with manufacturers of agricultural and other machinery.

There has been brewing at Cliff Brewery since 1746 when Cobbold & Co Ltd transferred there from Harwich. It was in 1957 that this brewery merged with Tollemache's Breweries Ltd, at whose brewery in Ipswich beer had been brewed since 1856, to form the present company. The subsidiary breweries at Cambridge and Walthamstow ceased production in 1972 and all brewing is now centred at Cliff Brewery.

RECOGNITION

There is at present a distinctive large Cambridge blue square or strip painted on the pub's wall on which 'Tolly Cobbold' or 'Tolly Cobbold Ales' or close variations is painted in dark red (usually) letters. There may be a hanging illuminated sign on which is written 'Tolly Cobbold Ales'. The trade marks are Cardinal Wolsey—who was born in Ipswich—and a bacchante, a priestess of the god of wine, Bacchus. The Bacchante is based on a statue that the Hon. Douglas Tollemache saw at the Paris exhibition in 1902 and bought for his garden.

TIED HOUSES

There are about 380 of these, nearly all of which are in the counties of Suffolk and Cambridgeshire. In Norfolk there are two Tolly Cobbold houses in Norwich (Pigeons, Wild Man) and one in Weasenham St Peter just south of Fakenham. In Essex there are two at Colchester (Buck's Horn, Bugle Horn); and in Oxford there is a leased house—the King's Arms.

There is a free trade throughout the trading area which is also extensive in Norfolk. Bottled beers are widely available in North London off-licences.

BEERS

Draught	Best Bitter. A distinctively flavoured brew which is well hopped.
	Mild. A dark beer.
	Old Strong. An old ale for the winter.
Keg	Tollykeg. A well hopped keg beer. Not

in all houses, the alternative being Worthington E keg beer.

Draught Lager (Husky). Brewed at Cliff Brewery.

Bottled   Light Bitter Ale. Well hopped with an agreeable flavour and quite well known outside the trading area.

Tolly Ale Export. Stronger and with a similar palate to the above.

Cardinal Ale. A yet stronger pale ale.

Tolly Royal Barley Wine.

Dark Brown Ale. A dry brown ale.

Cobnut. A sweet brown ale.

Double Stout. A medium sweet stout.

Some of Bass Charrington's beers are available through a trading agreement with that company.

Draught beers are dispensed by top pressure, manual bar pumps or direct from the cask.

79 TRUMAN LTD

'Truman—the real taste of flavour'

ADDRESS

91, Brick Lane, London E1. Tel 01-427-4300.

Trumans have been brewing in the heart of London's East End for over 300 years, and in 1972 a new brewing complex built on the same site commenced operations. The Truman dray-horses—Suffolk punches—which were a familiar and colourful site in the East End for many years have now been moved, because of the heavy traffic, to the Colchester area in the countryside of Essex where they may still be seen on local deliveries. Truman Ltd is part of the Grand

Metropolitan Hotels group, and operates 90 off-licences under the name of Gilbert Reeves who also ship and bottle their own wine under the name of Carabonne, Carabella and Carajo.

RECOGNITION

The Truman new look has become a familiar sight within the trading areas with its conspicuous orange and red stripes and circular symbol of various colours, which incorporates a T-shaped wheat sheaf and the date 1666 (when the brewery was founded). Truman pubs can be recognised by an octagonal illuminated sign featuring the symbol (orange with white letters) usually placed over the pub's door. There is also a board with an orange and red stripe either side of which is written 'Truman' in gold letters and the pub's name in white.

Other than as a wheatsheaf the new symbol has been interpreted in several ways but most commonly as a stylised T for Truman or as all roads leading to and from the brewery and the pubs.

TIED HOUSES

The majority of Truman's 1,100 or so licensed houses are in the Greater London area and the Home Counties. In central London Truman's beers may be found in Fleet St and near Trafalgar Square (St Martin's Lane). The most distant concentration of Truman pubs is in South Wales where there are just over 80 in the Swansea area. In the counties not far from London Truman's pubs may be found as follows:

In Essex. Widespread but especially in the Colchester area and also at Clacton, Canvey Island, Tilbury, Ilford, Loughton, Romford, Stanford-le-Hope, Woodford and Southend.

In Kent. Strong in the Gravesend area and also at Chatham, Northfleet, Margate and Ramsgate.

In Surrey. At Richmond, Wallington, Morden, Hurst Park, Thornton Heath, Redhill and Thames Ditton.

In Berkshire. At Reading, Maidenhead and Woodley.

In Hertfordshire. At Bishop's Stortford, St Albans area and Stevenage.

In Bedfordshire. One in Bedford and several in the county.

In Norfolk. At Norwich and Great Yarmouth.

In Suffolk. At Lowestoft and Ipswich.

There is an extensive free trade.

BEERS

Draught	Special Bitter. Medium gravity and quite well hopped.
	Mild Ale. Sweet and dark.
	Prize Brew. A low-gravity light mild which is mainly in the free trade and some of the Essex pubs. It is also available in a darker form.
	Ben Truman Export Draught. A new strong beer with a good flavour.
Keg	Tuborg Lager. The well-known Danish lager which is now being brewed at Brick Lane.
Bottled	Light Ale. Also in non-returnable bottles.

Ben Truman. A strong pale ale. Well hopped, as pointed out in the old advertising slogan—'There's more hops in Ben Truman'.

Export Light Ale. A strong light ale mainly for ship's stores and export but available in a few outlets in England. Between Light Ale and Ben Truman in strength.

Barley Wine. Matured for eight months before bottling.

Brown Ale. Medium sweet.

Eagle Stout. Also medium sweet.

Tuborg Lager.

Cans   Barbecue. In 4 and 7 pint cans and described as a light sparkling draught beer.

Other take-home packs are ¼ litre NRT bottles of brown ale and Tuborg Lager, and small cans of Ben Truman.

Guinness is available on 'draught' (ie keg), in bottle and small can.

Draught beers are dispensed by top pressure CO_2.

80a   VAUX AND ASSOCIATED BREWERIES LTD

'Brewed in the north for people who know good beer'
'Beers to boast about'

ADDRESS

The Brewery, Sunderland, Co Durham. Tel 56431.
There are two subsidiary breweries:

Vaux & Associated Breweries (80b), Caledonian Brewery, Slateford Rd, Edinburgh. It is here that Lorimer's Best Scotch Ale and 5 Star Strong Ale are brewed.

Thos. Usher & Son Ltd (80b), Park Brewery, 106 St Leonards St, Edinburgh. Tel 031-667-3311.

In addition Vaux own and operate the Swallow Hotel Group which has 19 comfortable town and country hotels in northern England, recognisable by the sign of the swallow. Some are in historic settings and others in the heart of Newcastle, Sunderland and Teesside. In Scotland the group has 10 town and country hotels and 10 well-known restaurants in Edinburgh, Glasgow and Aberdeen. The group's beers can be obtained at all these establishments.

Dray-horses are still in action, and fifteen Percherons are kept for local deliveries both in Sunderland and in Edinburgh.

Vaux Breweries

RECOGNITION

Vaux pubs are easily recognised by an illuminated yellow V-shaped sign with the name 'Vaux' in red over the doorway to the public bar. The pub sign carries a design, where it is considered to be appropriate, and the pub's name, together with that of the town, village or district (in large cities), where relevant.

TIED HOUSES

There are 700 of these in an area north of a line from

Whitby to Liverpool and up to the Scottish border.
Particularly strong on the east side of the area. The
first Vaux house going north on the A1 is at
Boroughbridge.

BEERS

Draught	Samson. A strong draught bitter mostly drunk in Teesside pubs and in the Tees Valley. Well-flavoured and not at all sweet.
	Lorimer Best Scotch. This is the draught bitter which is in all Vaux pubs except where Samson only is sold. It is a well-balanced beer.
	Pale Ale. A light bitter equivalent to a light mild. It is to be found mainly in smaller towns and villages where it is known as 'Ordinary'.
Keg	Gold Tankard. A strong keg beer.
	Silver Tankard. Medium gravity and darker and more bitter than the Gold Tankard.
	Norseman Lager. This is passed through a cooling unit.
Bottled	Special Export. A strong pale ale.
	5 Star Strong Ale. A barley wine.
	Light Brown Ale. A medium sweet ale approaching a low gravity pale ale in palate.
	Double Maxim. A strong brown ale. Darker and sweeter than the Special Export.
	Sweet Stout.
	Norseman Lager.

Canned   Double Maxim.
Golden Export. A strong pale ale from Ushers.
Norseman Lager.

Draught beers are mostly stored in stainless steel cellar tanks. A few houses have manual bar pumps or serve direct from casks. Otherwise they are dispensed by top pressure CO_2 and electric pumps to metered counter units. Keg beer is stored in 9 or 11 gallon kegs in the cellar and raised by top pressure.

Thos. Usher & Son Ltd

RECOGNITION

Outside the pub a hanging illuminated oval blue sign with a gold tankard in its centre. The pub's name is a neon sign on the facia of the pub, designed to suit the architecture.

TIED HOUSES

200 pubs spread over a wide area from Inverness in the north-east to the border with England, with the greatest number in and around Edinburgh.

BEERS

Keg   Export. The strongest of the keg beers.
Special Gold Tankard. The equivalent of a 'Keg Heavy' and approaching a bitter in quality.
Light. Of lower gravity and darker.
Norseman Lager.

Bottled	Golden Export. Strong and slightly sweet but with a pale ale flavour.
	Pale Ale. Lower gravity. A medium dark ale.
	Brown Ale. Dark and sweet like a bottled mild.
	Sweet Stout.
	Golden Lager.
Canned	Golden Export.
	Golden Lager.

81   WADWORTH & CO LTD

'Beer Brewed in the Traditional Manner'

ADDRESS

Northgate Brewery, Devizes, Wiltshire. Tel 3361-5.

Wadworth's massive red brick brewery, built in 1885, is a conspicuous feature of the town and dominates the market-place. The castle-like trade mark is the sign of the Northgate, which is the street in which the brewery was built. Wadworth's wine and spirit trade is provided by a chain of shops trading under the name of Edwin Giddings.

RECOGNITION

Colourful pictorial signs are most common, with 'Wadworth's' in gold lettering on a blue strip below the picture. 'Wadworths' is also usually written on the pub's wall.

TIED HOUSES

There are around 148 brewery-owned houses, most of which are in Wiltshire and lie in an area bounded by the road from Bath to Swindon (Wheatsheaf Hotel in Newport St), the road south to Amesbury, west to Warminster and back to Bath (Curfew Inn, Cleveland Place West; Long Acre Tavern, London Road). They are plentiful and easy to find within these boundaries. Outside this area Wadworth's beers can be found at Cricklade, Shrivenham, Faringdon and Aldbourne, all within a few miles of Swindon; and further north in the Burford area and on the edge of the Cotswolds at Burford, Witney, Carterton, Alvescot, Bampton and Clanfield. Further west Wadworth's ales are in Cheltenham (Cotswold Hotel in Portland St) and just south at Colesborne. Then towards Bristol at Dursley and Tetbury (on the Cirencester road); and around Bristol in Coalport Heath, Pucklechurch, Pilning, and to the south-west at Winford, Redhill and Blagdon. Also on the coast just north of Weston-super-Mare at Sand Bay and on the ring road at Gloucester. Further south and just north of Shaftesbury there are Wadworth houses at East Knoyle and Fonthill Gifford; and at Andover (Lamb Inn in Winchester St). The north-eastern outpost is at Stanton St John not far beyond Oxford.

There is an extensive free trade extending from Cheltenham to Bournemouth and Reading to Weston-super-Mare.

Wadworth produce a colourful brochure which lists the pubs.

BEERS

Draught   PA (Pale Ale). A distinctive bitter with

the taste of malt and hops.

IPA (India Pale Ale). Slightly stronger than the PA.

One of the above two beers (usually the IPA) is in every Wadworth pub.

6X. This is a strong bitter and at the least equivalent to a 'Best Bitter'. Also well flavoured and not at all sweet.

OT (Old Timer). A pale, very strong bitter, not now confined only to the winter months on draught.

Mild Ale. A dark beer.

Keg	Golden Keg. A high-gravity keg bitter.
Canned	Take-home 4 pt cans of bitter and OT. The bitter is the same beer as used for bottled Pale Ale but with less CO_2. The OT is filtered and pasteurised.
Bottled	Pale Ale.
	Green Label. A strong pale ale.
	Old Timer 'Special Country Brew'. A very strong pale ale from the same basic brew as the draught and canned OT.
	Brown Ale. Medium sweet.
	Middy Brown. A stronger brown ale and sweeter.
	Oatmeal Stout. A dryish stout.

Draught beers are dispensed predominantly from wooden casks direct or via manual bar pumps. There is a top-pressure system in some pubs. The wooden casks may be enclosed by a water jacket to keep them cool in hot weather.

82   S.H. WARD & CO LTD

'Fine Malt Ales'

ADDRESS

Sheaf Brewery, Ecclesall Road, Sheffield, Yorkshire.
Tel 78787/8/9.

RECOGNITION

Bright red signs with black letters. The house trade
mark is generally 'Welcome to Wards' above or below
a gold barley sheaf. 'Ward's Fine Malt Ales' is
frequently written on the sign or the pub's wall.

TIED HOUSES

Most of the company's licensed houses, upwards of
100, are in Sheffield and surroundings, but a 'Wel-
come to Wards' can be found also much further afield.
Look for the Ward signs in Lincolnshire at Retford
and as far east as Brigg and district, Barton-on-
Humber and Louth. In Derbyshire as far south as
Ilkeston (between Derby and Nottingham), at Hors-
ley Woodhouse (near Heanor) and Ripley on the
Derby-Chesterfield road. Also at Froggatt Edge and
Bakewell (west of Chesterfield), and Peak Forest just
north-east of Buxton. North of Sheffield there are
Ward houses at Grenoside, Chapeltown, Hoyland,
Blacker Hill and Oxspring in the Sheffield/Barnsley
area, and as far north as Sowerby Bridge near Halifax
(Puzzle Hall).

BEERS

Draught   Bitter. A beer with a distinct character-
               istic and malty flavour.

	BB Best Bitter. A higher gravity bitter.
	Mild Ale. A light mild with an agreeable flavour.
Bottled	Pale Ale.
	Brown Ale.
	Kirby Ale. A stronger brown ale.
	Welcome Stout.

Draught beers are dispensed by metered electric pumps but a few houses still have manual bar pumps.

83   CHARLES WELLS LTD

'Wells' Bedford Ales'

ADDRESS

The Brewery, Bedford, Beds. Tel 51821.

Bedford is a river town on the Great Ouse by which stands the brewery, near the road bridge in from the south. It is 51 miles north of London and 29 miles west of Cambridge.

RECOGNITION

'Charles Wells' is written in a red band beneath the inn-sign painting. Symbols on the pub's wall are 'Wells' Bedford Ales', 'A Charles Wells House', or 'Charles Wells Ltd'. Part of the Bedford town coat of arms—an eagle—is portrayed on a plaque on the front walls of the pubs by the door.

TIED HOUSES

Along or inside an imaginary line along the road from

Northampton (here there are the Duke of Edinburgh, and the Headland) to Kettering (Cherry Tree), then to Huntingdon (The Territorial), Cambridge (Ancient Druids, Elm Tree, Wrestlers), Luton (Compasses, Green Man, White Lion) and then along the A5 to Towcester and back to Northampton, you are in the thick of Charles Wells country. There are around 270 Wells houses and they overflow outside the above region as follows. Starting north of Towcester and going clockwise, places with Wells pubs are: Stowe Hill, Gayton, Daventry (Golden Hind), Norton, East Haddon, Clipston, Brixworth, Harrington, Rothwell, Thorpe, Titchmarsh, Thriplow, Hitchin (Bricklayer's Arms, Fountain), Charlton, Harpenden (Silver Cup), Cheddington, Mentmore, Leighton Buzzard (Ashwell Arms, White Lion), Great Brickhill, Bletchley (Dolphin, in Whaddon Way), Padbury, Poundon, Buckingham (the Swan & Castle Hotel), Brackley (Red Lion), Helmdon, Deanshanger and back to Towcester where there are several.

A map of the pubs with other information has been prepared by the company.

BEERS

Draught	IPA. A well hopped draught bitter.
	Mild. A darkish nutty-flavoured beer.
Keg	Noggin Keg. Also above average in hopping rate and well flavoured.
	Ace Lager.
Bottled	Light Ale.
	Star Special. A strong bottled bitter.
	Fargo Ale—export quality. A strong ale.
	Old Bedford Ale. A barley wine.

Brown Ale. Similar to the mild.
Welcome Brown. A sweet brown ale.
Bowman Stout. Medium sweet.
Draught beers are mainly dispensed by top pressure but some houses still serve by means of manual bar pumps or direct from cask.

84 THE WOLVERHAMPTON & DUDLEY BREWERIES LTD

'Traditional draught beer from the cask'

ADDRESS

Park Brewery, Wolverhampton, Staffs. Tel 21201.
   There are two operating breweries:

Wolverhampton & Dudley Breweries Ltd, Park Brewery, Wolverhampton, which trades under the name of *Banks's.*
Julia Hanson & Sons Ltd, High St and Greystone St, Dudley, which trades under the name of *Hanson's.*

RECOGNITION

The standard sign is square-shaped with a rectangular white base and a black or chocolate semi-circular background. On this is superimposed a white lion with 'Banks's' or 'Hansons' in yellow. There may be an illuminated pole or bracket sign in white with the pub's name underneath in yellow. Sometimes there is a flat shield sign on the wall. 'Banks's' or 'Hansons' may also be written on the pub's wall.

TIED HOUSES

There are approximately 800 licensed houses between the two companies as follows.

Banks's

Predominantly on a line between Wolverhampton and Kidderminster and spreading out on both sides. Outposts are at Coventry, Great Malvern, Hereford, Worcester, Tenbury Wells, Bridgnorth, Stafford and Leicester. Also north-west into Shropshire at Shrewsbury, Newport and Oswestry, and into Mid Wales to Welshpool and the coast. Banks houses can easily be found in and around the above places.

Hanson's

Centred at Dudley and all stations south to Kidderminster, and at Worcester and Great Malvern.

The company has free trade interests.

BEERS

Banks's

Draught	Bitter. A well hopped draught beer. Mild. A light mild which is also well hopped.
Bottled	Banks's Bitter. A pale ale. Old Ale. A very strong dark ale of barley wine type. Banks's Brown Ale. Mild Ale. A mild ale in bottle.
Cans	Foursome Bitter and Foursome Mild in 4 pint cans.

Hanson's

Draught   Bitter. A pale draught beer slightly more
            hoppy in flavour than Banks's.
            Mild. A light-coloured well hopped mild
            ale.
Bottled   Hanson's Special Stout. Medium sweet.
            Banks's bottled beers are also sold in
            Hanson's pubs.

Draught beers are all naturally conditioned in the
cask in the cellar and are mainly dispensed by electric
pumps and meter dispensers on the counter. In some
cases manual bar pumps are still in use. The Porter
Lancastrian system with compressed air and a light
top pressure is adopted in some pubs.

85   WORKINGTON BREWERY CO LTD

'John Peel Cumberland Ales'

ADDRESS

The Brewery, Workington, Cumberland. Tel 2677/8.
    Workington is a seaport on the Solway coast at the
estuary of the river Derwent. It makes steel, wood
pulp and buses, and extrudes aluminium.
    John Peel Ales have been brewed in Workington
since 1792 and the trade name is taken from the
Cumberland fell huntsman who is immortalised in the
famous hunting song 'D'ye ken John Peel'. The
brewery, originally built in 1792, was partly rebuilt
and extended in 1892 and whilst retaining a picturesque and traditional tower brewery appearance
from outside is completely modern within. There is a

wine and spirit department which ships a comprehensive range of wines to the free trade in the Lake
District.

RECOGNITION

There is either a pictorial sign beneath which a red
title strip reads 'A John Peel House', or a red
illuminated sign bearing the company's trade mark of
the John Peel head and shoulders motif in gold with
the title 'John Peel Ales'. The house colours make an
attractive combination with the red John Peel signs—
white stone-work with grey sills and pale blue
woodwork.

TIED HOUSES

John Peel Ales may be drunk in 110 tied houses
spread over Cumberland, Westmorland and part of
North Lancashire. The main trading area is within the
industrial belt of West Cumberland but it also extends
south to Grange-over-Sands, Barrow-in-Furness and
Millom. Then in the Lake District at Bowness-on-
Windermere, Keswick and surroundings, and further
east at Penrith. The Cumberland huntsman sign can
also be seen in most of the smaller towns and villages
in Cumberland and is easy to detect.

There is a free trade and a service depot across the
Solway at Dumfries which caters for much of
south-west Scotland.

BEERS

Draught   John Peel XXX Best Bitter. An agreeable

	malty flavour.
	John Peel 'Barley Brown' Best Mild. A dark nutty beer.
Keg	John Peel Golden Bitter. A strong keg bitter with a delicate flavour.
Bottled	John Peel Pale Ale.
	John Peel Export Ale. A strong pale ale.
	John Peel Brown Ale. Nutty in flavour.
	John Peel Stout. A sweet stout.

Draught beers are dispensed by manual bar pumps or electric pumps.

86   YATES & JACKSON LTD

ADDRESS

Brock St, Lancaster, Lancs. Tel 2860.

The brewery is in Brewery Lane and has the date 1669 on a stone over the entrance.

RECOGNITION

Usually there is just the name of the pub, but new signs are being introduced for the pub wall on which is written 'Yates & Jackson Ltd'.

TIED HOUSES

There are 43 of these within a 25-mile radius of Lancaster, most of which are in Lancaster and Morecambe and points between. There are 5 in the centre of Morecambe—in Queen St and nearby. They can also be found as follows:

To the north. The Globe in the Market Place at Kendal.

To the south. About 10 miles south of Lancaster on the A6. There are 8 in this area.

At Overton. Two in this village just south of Lancaster near the coast.

At Ingleton and nearby. This is in Yorkshire on the edge of the Dales and just off the A65. There are 4 around here.

BEERS

Draught	Bitter. A good well hopped draught beer.
	Mild. A dark, not too sweet mild.
Bottled	Pale Ale. Similar to the bitter.
	Nut Brown. A medium sweet brown ale.

Draught beers—all from wooden casks—are dispensed in about half the pubs by manual bar pumps and in the other half by electric pumps and counter dispensers.

87   YORKSHIRE CLUBS' BREWERY LTD

ADDRESS

New Lane, Huntington, York. Tel York 22837.

Huntington is on the north-eastern outskirts of the city.

SOME HISTORY AND FACTS OF INTEREST

As with the other two clubs' breweries, the Yorkshire Clubs' brewery was conceived near the end of World War I because of what clubmen considered unfair treatment of clubs by brewers during the war years. The York branch of the Working Men's Club & Institute Union Ltd decided to form a brewery after an unsuccessful attempt to obtain more favourable trading conditions from the brewers. But there were many problems—money, transport, equipment—and after eighteen months only £748 had been raised. In the meantime a redundant brewery was found which the owner put into the necessary condition for brewing. This was rented on a 10-year lease with the option to purchase, and with only £748 capital brewing commenced. Needless to say, incidents of tribulation were many but eventually the Clubs' Brewery organisation triumphed and a new modern brewery was built on the present site at Huntington. Later, the Leeds Clubs' Brewery was amalgamated with the York Clubs' Brewery under the name of the Yorkshire Clubs' Brewery Ltd and all operations were centred at Huntington.

TRADING AREAS

The Clubs' Brewery now supplies well over 200 clubs all over Yorkshire except the Cleveland area (this is most of Teesside), into Lancashire, Derbyshire, Nottinghamshire and Lincolnshire. Supplies have now commenced in the Midlands.

BEERS

Draught   6X, 4X and Light Bitter are all well-flavoured bitters with a high hopping rate. They are in descending order of strength.
Dark Mild. A dark beer equivalent in strength to the Light Bitter.
Best Mild. Equivalent to the 4X in strength.

Bottled   4X, Bitter and Special are all pale ales. The Special is the strongest.

CB Brown. A medium sweet brown ale. Draught beers are dispensed by manual bar pumps, electric pumps or top pressure, according to the particular club's requirements.

88   YOUNG & CO'S BREWERY LTD

'Real Draught Beer'

ADDRESS

The Ram Brewery, Wandsworth, London SW18. Tel 01-870-0141/5.

A team of 24 shire horses is still kept for deliveries of beer within a three-mile radius of the brewery. These are the kind or horses that were used hundreds of years ago to carry knights in armour into battle. The Young & Co horses are black with white 'socks' and weigh over a ton each.

RECOGNITION

'Young & Co' is usually written in conspicuous letters on the pub's wall. 'Young' pubs can also be identified by the company trade mark which is a ram. Most houses have hanging pictorial signs.

TIED HOUSES

There are nearly 140 of these with the biggest concentration in south-west London, and south of the river Thames within and along a line from Walton-on-Thames, through Epsom, Sutton, Croydon and Chislehurst. Outside this area look for the sign of the ram at Chertsey; further into the country at Gomshall and Shere (Surrey); Walton-on-the-Hill also in Surrey; and as far south as Plumpton Green in Sussex, north-west of Lewes. North of the Thames there are Young houses at Barking, Dalston, Greenford (on Western Avenue), Hackney, Hampstead, Harlesden, Homerton, Kilburn and Stepney. Nearer central London in Bow St, Petty France (Westminster), Albert St (Regent's Park), Bruton Place (off Berkeley Sq), Kensington (in Allen St and Warwick Rd) and Lamb's Conduit St in Holborn.

Once within a Young pub, the others will be very easy to find, because a folder is supplied to the pubs listing them all with their addresses.

There is a free trade which extends well beyond the tied house area.

BEERS

Draught	Ordinary Bitter. Very well hopped with an agreeable flavour.
	Special Bitter. Stronger and slightly sweeter than the 'Ordinary'.
	Best Malt Ale. A dark mild beer.
	Winter Warmer or Old Ale. A strong dark ale for winter only.
Keg	Young's Keg Bitter.
	Saxon Lager.
Bottled	Pale Ale.
	Ram Rod. A strong pale ale.
	Strong Export Bitter. A very strong pale

ale brewed specially for the Belgian market where Young & Co have trading connections.

Old Nick. A barley wine.

Brown Ale. Medium sweet.

Saxon Lager.

Draught beers are dispensed by manual bar pumps or in a few cases direct from the cask.

CHAPTER 8

The National Brewers

The 'Big Seven' national brewers are Allied Breweries Ltd, Bass Charrington Ltd, Courage Ltd, Arthur Guinness Son & Co Ltd, Scottish & Newcastle Breweries Ltd, Watney Mann Ltd, and Whitbread & Co Ltd. There is very little difficulty in locating the pubs of any of them. Nevertheless they do have areas of comparative weakness, as they also have areas where they may be very strong, perhaps to the exclusion of other brewers. So some indication is given under each brewer (except Guinness, which distributes in the free trade and in the pubs of all other brewers) as to the spheres of influence.

The pattern is much the same as with the regional brewers, although the beers are in some cases divided into those distributed on a national basis and those that can be found only in certain regions. Some of the lesser known regional beers may not be included, as rationalisation is a frequent phenomenon and some of the local beers are continually disappearing.

'Facts and figures about the group' include the size of the organisation, how it developed out of a series of amalgamations, and related companies within the group.

How to recognise the pubs is explained and, where appropriate, the signs of a local company which may have been taken over but can still be recognised (eg Friary Meux, Samuel Webster, John Smith, and others).

ALLIED BREWERIES LTD

REGISTERED OFFICE

Allied House, 156 St John Street, London, EC1. Tel 01-253-9911.

FACTS AND FIGURES ABOUT THE GROUP

Allied Breweries Ltd is the largest and broadest-based drinks company in Europe (including wines, spirits and soft drinks) with some 8,000 pubs in England and Wales. It was founded in 1961 through the merger of three companies—Ind Coope, Tetley Walker and Ansells. The group has a wide drinks interest with its subsidiaries Harveys (wines and sherries), Showerings (Babycham), Britvic Fruit Juices, and Coates, Gaymers and Whiteways (ciders). It owns two Dutch brewery companies—D'Oranjeboom and Breda—and a chain of 48 hotels.

There are eight operating breweries in Britain at present. Six of these are for ale—at Burton-on-Trent, Birmingham (2), Leeds, Warrington and Romford. Two are for lager—at Wrexham and Alloa. Eleven per cent of the pubs in Britain are owned by Allied, which is the second largest beer producer in the United Kingdom with over 15 per cent of the market for beer. The brewery at Burton is, at present, the largest ale brewery in Europe and is where all the Double Diamond is brewed.

RECOGNITION

Ind Coope

Orange signboards with a plaque on the pub's wall depicting a hand within a glass in black and red. There are approximately 2,220 pubs covering the south of England below a line running from the Severn estuary to the north Norfolk coast, plus a further 800 or more within greater London. In parts of Surrey and Sussex many Ind Coope pubs still have the red and black signboards of Friary Meux, the old Guildford brewery. Similarly in Hertfordshire there are still some Benskins (Watford brewery) signs, and here and in Buckinghamshire around Aylesbury red signs (ABC—The Aylesbury Brewery Co is now part of the group).

Ansells

The sign is a beer barrel within a black square, and the top half of the barrel depicts a white squirrel on a green background. The bottom half is orange on which 'Ansells the better beer' is written. There are 1,890 pubs concentrated in the industrial Midlands with others covering the Midlands and Wales from the Ind Coope trading area to a line between Liverpool Bay and the Humber Estuary. There are still some Ind Coope pubs in the Midlands, but these will eventually become Ansells.

Tetley

The red-coated huntsman sign can be seen to the north in Yorkshire and Lancashire and up to the Scottish border. The main concentration is in the West Riding of Yorkshire where there are 940 pubs, and in the Liverpool-Manchester area where there are 1,150 and where the most familiar sign outside them is a rider on horseback (ex Walker of Warrington).

The remaining 25 per cent of the total is outside the areas of concentration named above. In Scotland, Allied's beers are sold through the free trade.

A new corporate symbol is being introduced based on a stylised 'glass' for Allied Breweries (UK) Ltd. The regional identifications (a hand, a squirrel and a huntsman) are included within that glass for use on pubs in their areas.

BEERS

Draught. A bitter and a dark mild are brewed in each of the three main trading areas. In Ind Coope pubs they are known as Super Draught Bitter and Super Draught Mild and have a sweetish palate. Double Diamond is a keg beer with a sweet palate and is Allied's leading brand which is brewed exclusively at Burton-on-Trent. It was introduced on draught in 1962 and has the largest sales of a keg beer in Britain. It can also be obtained in 4 pint cans. Skol International Lager is the draught lager. Long Life is on draught in some pubs in London and the south-east. It is brewed in a manner similar to lager but in taste is intentionally positioned midway between beer and lager.

National

| Bottled & cans | Ind Coope Light Ale. Also in NRT (non-returnable) bottles. |

Ind Coope Light Ale. Also in NRT (non-returnable) bottles.

Ind Coope Brown Ale. Also in NRT bottles.

Double Diamond. In bottles, half pint cans and NRT bottles.

Triple A. A strong ale similar to a barley wine. Not too sweet.

Long Life. In cans only.

Skol International Lager. In bottles, cans and NRT bottles.

Oranjeboom de Luxe Lager. Imported from the Dutch subsidiary in bottle only and available at a limited number of outlets.

Caskette. Take home 4 pint cans containing a 'draught' bitter.

Regional

Bottled light and brown ales are brewed for Ansell and Tetley houses. Caskette is available in the Midlands also as a fairly dark mild beer.

BASS CHARRINGTON LTD

REGISTERED OFFICE

54-60 Baker Street, London, W1. Tel 01-486 1277

FACTS AND FIGURES ABOUT THE GROUP

Bass Charrington is the largest brewing business in

Europe with twenty breweries at present and over 10,000 pubs, hotels and off-licences. It is the largest supplier of beer in Britain and is strongly represented in wines and spirits through Bass Charrington Vintners which either owns or has the agency for such brands as Bacardi Rum, Mouton Cadet Claret, Emva Cream Cyprus Sherry, Ruffino Chianti, Old Bushmills Irish Whiskey, Vat 69 Scotch Whisky, Mateus Rose and the Bolla range of Italian wines. Its soft drinks subsidiary is Canada Dry (UK). Over 80 hotels in England and Wales are owned through its subsidiary Crest Hotels Ltd.

Bass Charrington was formed in 1967 by the merger of Charrington United Breweries and Bass, Mitchells and Butlers; each of which was the result of a series of mergers. For Charrington it all started at Mile End in the eighteenth century, and after a series of acquisitions the company merged with United Breweries of York in 1962 to become CUB—Charrington United Breweries. For Bass, Mitchells and Butlers it all goes back to Bass & Co founded in 1777 and Worthington & Co founded in 1744, both at Burton-on-Trent. At one time the Baltic trade accounted for nearly all the output of Bass and Worthington. It was cheaper to ship their beer by sea than to send it by road to London and the south. Then in 1822 a crippling tariff caused a switch of markets to India and Asia, and India Pale Ale came into being. It was by accident that Bass came to be sold widely in Britain—a ship bound for the East was wrecked in the Irish Sea and the salvaged cargo included casks of Bass which made such an impression on local palates that people wanted more. By 1869 Bass was trading as Bass, Ratcliffe & Gretton and that was the name under which Bass and Worthington amalgamated when they merged in 1926. The company then merged with Mitchells and Butlers of Birmingham in 1961 to form Bass, Mitchells and Butlers.

RECOGNITION

The well-known house sign—an orange Toby jug on a bright red triangle—can be seen throughout England and Wales on all Bass Charrington houses. The red triangle is the original trade mark of Bass and is the oldest registered trade mark in the world. It dates back to 1875 when registration became compulsory under the Trade Mark Act of that date. The Toby jug originates from the Charrington half of the group. The doors on most pubs are the same bright red as the triangle. In Scotland, Bass Charrington is represented by its subsidiary Tennent Caledonian Breweries Ltd of Glasgow, and its pubs can be identified by a conspicuous red T. Many pubs in South Wales still have Hancock signboards.

BEERS

Familiar names to beer drinkers are those of Bass and Worthington and both these brand names are given to a series of beers—draught bitter, keg beers, bottled beers and beers in can. The well-known name of Worthington E originated from a cask bitter, brewed in the traditional way, from Burton-on-Trent, and it is still available over a wide area, often in free houses. Worthington E is now mostly sold in keg form.
Widely distributed bottled beers are:

> White Label. This is naturally conditioned and has a slight sediment in the bottle.

Bass Blue Triangle.

Worthington E.

Both of these are pale ales and are synonymous.

Bass Export. A strong pale ale.

No 1 Barley Wine.

Toby Brown. A medium sweet brown ale.

Jubilee Stout. A sweet stout.

Carling Black Label. The English version of the well-known Canadian lager. In bottle, can and keg (England and Wales).

Tennent's Lager. In bottle, can and keg (in Scotland).

Widely distributed regional beers are Brew Ten in the North and Brew Eleven in the Midlands, both in keg and draught form; and Crown Bitter—a draught bitter for the South East.

M & B Mild, sold widely in the Midlands, is a medium pale mild not unlike some bitters. There is also a selection of local beers often under the names of Bass and Worthington or Tennent in Scotland. Several local beers are still brewed, such as in Cardiff for the South Wales market by Welsh Brewers Ltd. Well-known brands locally are Stones Bitter from Sheffield and Highgate Mild in the Walsall area of the Midlands.

There are a number of other local beers which are not mentioned here because of continual changes and rationalisation.

COURAGE LTD

REGISTERED OFFICE

Anchor Terrace, Southwark Bridge, London, SE1. Tel 01-407-7676.

FACTS AND FIGURES ABOUT THE GROUP

The Courage group was formed by the merger of a number of brewery companies. The London brewers Courage & Co Ltd joined Barclay Perkins & Co Ltd in 1955 to form Courage & Barclay Ltd. They were joined by H & G Simonds Ltd of Reading in 1960, and by Bristol Brewery Georges & Co Ltd in 1961. The company then became known as Courage, Barclay & Simonds Ltd. In 1970 John Smith's Tadcaster Brewery Co Ltd joined the group which then became known as Courage Ltd. Since then—in 1971—the Plymouth Breweries Ltd have been acquired.

The group consists of four main divisions. *Courage (Eastern) Ltd* with a brewery in London (Horselydown by Tower Bridge) and with over 1,700 licensed houses covering South East England and East Anglia. *Courage (Central) Ltd* trading over central southern England and brewing at Reading with more than 1,200 pubs. *Courage (Western) Ltd* which trades over all of western England and a large part of Wales (South and Mid). It controls nearly 1,300 public houses with its main brewery at Bristol. It also has two breweries at Plymouth which are administered by Courage PB Ltd and who look after Courage (Western) interests in Devon and Cornwall and have a further 450 pubs and off-licences. *John Smith's Tadcaster Brewery Co Ltd* which trades over most of northern England and down to the Midlands with some 1,700 public houses. It has breweries at Tadcaster near York (John Smith), Barnsley and Newark (Hole).

In all, there are eight operating breweries and the main canning plant is at Alton in Hampshire. The group owns nearly 7,000 licensed houses.

There are also a number of other subsidiary companies in the group such as Anchor Hotels and Taverns with 24 hotels and banqueting establishments in the south, and Acorn Hotels in the north. In wines and spirits there is Saccone & Speed, Charles Kinloch & Co Ltd and Arthur Cooper (Wine Merchant) Ltd. Courage have an interest in Harp Lager with four breweries; in Cantrell & Cochrane (Great Britain) Ltd—soft drinks; and in The Taunton Cider Co Ltd. There is a flourishing export trade and there are breweries at Melbourne, Australia; Belgium; and Spain in which Courage has an interest.

Courage is now owned by Imperial Tobacco Group Ltd.

RECOGNITION

The bright red sign boards with a Golden Cockerel superimposed are a familiar sight in the south of England. Here also many of the pubs have a blue board on the wall with the pub's name in gold. In the South West many of the houses have the letters PB in red or 'a PB house'. In the north look for the sign of the red and blue magnet (John Smith) usually with 'Magnet Ales' written on the pub's wall. Other houses have green signboards advertising Barnsley Bitter (ex Warwick & Richardson houses; Barnsley pub signs were red and white) and around Newark others still have 'Hole's Ales' on the pub's wall.

BEERS

Draught   Courage Best Bitter. A well hopped traditional bitter from the cask, brewed regionally to suit local palates. Also known as Top Draught (usually with newer dispensers).

PBA Pale Bitter Ale. A lightish bitter mainly in the South East.

Full Brew. A bitter brewed in Bristol.

Directors Bitter. A strong cask bitter served in a number of pubs in the South East, with a good 'fruity' flavour.

Plymouth Heavy. An agreeable dry mild in the South West.

John Smith's Bitter.

Barnsley Bitter.

These are traditional bitters in the north which are increasingly served from cellar tanks.

Hole's AK. A bitter from Newark.

Keg
Tavern. This is the group's nationally distributed beer from the keg, which has a distinct smack of hops.

Draught John Courage. A new strong bitter introduced in December 1972 and equivalent to bottled John Courage.

Special IPA. A keg beer from Courage (Central) Ltd of bland flavour.

PB Superkeg Mild. A dark mild from Plymouth.

There are also a number of other draught bitters and light and dark milds brewed locally.

Bottled
Courage Light Ale. Nationally distributed.

Magnet Pale. A strongish pale ale from the north.

John Courage. A strong pale ale.

Bulldog Pale Ale. A yet stronger PA.

Magnet Old. A strong dark ale from Tadcaster.

Courage Barley Wine.

Russian Imperial Stout. This is one of the strongest beers brewed. It is conditioned in bottle for at least two years and acquired its name in the eighteenth century when it was admired by the then Empress of Russia.

Courage Brown Ale. Medium sweet.

Velvet Stout. Also medium sweet.

There are a number of other locally brewed bottled beers.

Canned   There are a number of these including the Jackpot, a party-size can of draught beer (something like the PBA) for the home.

There are a variety of dispensing systems in Courage pubs.

ARTHUR GUINNESS SON & CO LTD

REGISTERED OFFICE

Park Royal Brewery, London, NW10. Tel 01-965-7700.

FACTS AND FIGURES ABOUT GUINNESS

Guinness is a unique product in the world of brewing in that its distribution is entirely via the free trade and the tied houses of other brewers. Guinness do not own a single tied house in the normal sense, although they do own the Castle Inn at Bodiam in East Sussex near the Kent border; but it is just like any free house and sells a variety of beers. It is right alongside Guinness territory—their own hop farms. Guinness has achieved its wide acceptance—essential with no tied outlets—because of its consistent quality and individual character over the years, and since 1929 has been supported by entertaining advertising campaigns. It is a naturally conditioned beer with a dry palate and creamy head.

It all started in 1759 when Arthur Guinness bought a brewery in Dublin. Today this brewery is one of the largest in Europe and its products are marketed in more than 140 different countries. In Great Britain there are still about 300 Guinness bottlers.

From its beginning in Dublin there are now five breweries as follows.

1. The St James's Gate Brewery, Dublin, which brews every kind of Guinness and supplies one-third of the British market, roughly the northern half, and those overseas markets where there is no local brewing of Guinness.
2. The Park Royal Brewery in London which was opened in 1936 and brews the two home market products—Extra Stout and Draught Guinness. Park Royal supplies the southern half of England.
3. The Ikeja Brewery, Nigeria, which was opened in 1963 and produces Foreign Extra Stout for the Nigerian market.
4. The Sungei Way Brewery at Kuala Lumpur, opened in 1966 to produce Foreign Extra Stout and later on also Gold Harp Lager.
5. Guinness Cameroun SA, opened at Douala, Cameroun, West Africa, in May 1970, produces Foreign Extra Stout and in future a lager will also be brewed.

A further brewery came into operation in Ghana in 1972.

Guinness is also brewed under contract in seven other countries overseas.

In 1960 Guinness launched a lager in Ireland called Harp. As this was successful it was introduced into Great Britain and a brewery for its production was built at Alton, Hampshire, in 1963. Harp Lager Ltd is owned today by Guinness 50 per cent, Courage 25 per cent and Scottish and Newcastle Breweries 25 per cent, and is brewed at Dundalk, Alton, Manchester and Edinburgh.

Great care is taken to ensure that the Guinness brewed in Great Britain and Ireland is identical. There is one exception to this in that Draught Guinness in Ireland has an even bigger head to suit local preference.

'Draught' (keg) Guinness is dispensed from metal casks by means of a special tap which gives it its characteristic head. It is extracted from the cask by the use of gas which is contained in an integral part of the cask. Therefore no gas cylinder is required and no adjustment of gas pressure is necessary on the part of the licensee or barman.

BEERS

Guinness is made by a natural process unchanged fundamentally since its inception. Uniformity is achieved by a blending of several different brewings. The use of some roasted barley gives it its characteristic dark colour.

Different strengths are produced to suit overseas markets and the following names are used to describe Guinness products.

Guinness Extra Stout. This is the familiar Guinness in bottle sold throughout Great Britain and Ireland. It is despatched in bulk to brewers and bottlers throughout the country who bottle it and allow it to condition by the action of the live yeast it contains. Being naturally conditioned in bottle, no CO_2 has to be introduced. It is available both in traditional and non-returnable bottles. Canned Guinness is also on sale.

Draught Guinness. This is also virtually confined to Great Britain and Ireland. The Guinness is conditioned in bulk prior to being filled into casks and despatched from the brewery.

Porter. A less strong draught brew, now on sale only in Northern Ireland.

Foreign Extra Stout. The strongest form with a very dry palate—even drier than the others. Brewed in Dublin, Malaysia, Nigeria and the Cameroons. Also under licence and direct technical control in several other countries.

Export Stout. As strong as Foreign Extra Stout but less dry. It is for export to Europe and for ship's stores trade.

Extra Stout for Export. This has a similar flavour to Extra Stout and is specially prepared for export markets including the USA.

Take-home packs of one-trip bottles are now widely available.

SCOTTISH & NEWCASTLE BREWERIES LTD

REGISTERED OFFICE

Abbey Brewery, Holyrood Road, Edinburgh. Tel 031-556-2591. There are two subsidiary brewing companies:

Scottish Brewers Ltd, at the group's registered office in Edinburgh.

The Newcastle Breweries Ltd, The Tyne Brewery, Gallowgate, Newcastle-upon-Tyne 1. Tel 25091.

Newcastle has always been a famous town for brewing and it has been said that it was the first town in England to perform that delicate and skilled operation. Perhaps Edinburgh has been even more prominent as a brewing town, with its particularly suitable supply of water from a number of wells on the northern slopes of the Pentlands and in the Duddingston area.

FACTS AND FIGURES ABOUT THE GROUP

Some famous brewing names are associated with the group. One of these was William Younger who established a brewery in Leith in 1749 which later moved to the precincts of Holyrood Abbey near the present Holyrood Brewery. The familiar Father William character with the top hat, long white beard and pint mug was the company's trade mark. Another famous name was William McEwan who commenced brewing in 1856 on the outskirts of Edinburgh at Fountainbridge. The equally familiar Cavalier figure became its trade mark. These two companies merged in 1931 to form Scottish Brewers Ltd and a number of other well-known Scottish Brewers were absorbed into the company including Robert Younger. In 1960, Scottish Brewers Ltd merged with The New-castle Breweries Ltd—with the blue star trade mark—to form the present company.

The group owns and operates three breweries—at Holyrood and Fountainbridge in Edinburgh, and the Tyne Brewery in Newcastle. All McEwan's and Younger's beers sold anywhere in the world are brewed in Edinburgh and all Newcastle beers are brewed on Tyneside. Harp Lager is brewed at the new Harp Lager Brewery in Holyrood. In addition there is an £11 million New Fountain Brewery being built at Fountainbridge which will be one of the largest and most automated in the world.

The group owns approximately 2,000 licensed premises in the United Kingdom including about 1,700 public houses the majority of which are managed. There are also 100 hotels, 25 of which are Thistle Hotels—the premier hotels of the group. The remainder of the licensed premises are made up of restaurants and off-licences. Scottish & Newcastle's policy is for managed houses to supply food, unless there is no demand, and in pursuance of this policy there is a chain of 'Bere 'n' Byte' operations in which a quick hot snack or a complete meal are offered. The company are establishing a chain of pubs in England called 'The Swinging Sporrans' and some of the traditional Scottish dishes such as Haggis, mash and neeps (turnip) are served. The Scottish flavour pre-dominates and the barmaids wear tartan mini-kilts. At present there are four Swinging Sporrans—at Oadby near Leicester; Islington, London; Sackville St, Man-chester; and Runcorn to the south of Liverpool.

Spirits and wine interests are served by the subsidiary company Mackinlay—McPherson Ltd which markets a number of brands including 'Mac-Kinlay's' Old Scotch Whisky, McPherson's 'Cluny' Scotch Whisky, 'Windjammer' Demerara Rum, the 'Timpano' range of sherries and the 'La Tour Clerac' and 'Prinz Rupprecht' ranges of table wines.

TRADING AREAS

The traditional trading areas are Scotland and northeast England, but the company is now extending its operations to cover the whole of the United Kingdom. There are 50 William Younger houses in London, and the free trade absorbs nearly two-thirds of the group's beer production. More than 50 per cent of beer brewed in Scotland is consumed in England and Wales. There is an export trade which includes Belgium, Canada, Chile, Gibraltar, Jamaica, Pakistan, South Africa, Spain and the USA, also NAAFI business, especially in Germany, ship's stores and British embassies.

RECOGNITION

The company sells its beers under the brand names of 'McEwan' (the Cavalier figure), 'William Younger' (Father William) and 'Newcastle'. Pubs belonging to the Newcastle brewery have a conspicuous blue star hanging outside. Scottish & Newcastle managed houses display all the above symbols together with the initials S & N. Thistle hotels display a green thistle sign; Scottish & Newcastle hotels a symbol depicting two bridges; and 'Bere 'n' Byte' houses Father William wearing a chef's hat.

BEERS

Draught (cask & cellar tank beers)

    Wm. McEwan's   60/-.

    Wm. McEwan's   70/-.

    Wm. McEwan's 80/-.

    These are classed by traditional brewer's marks or symbols and are in ascending order of gravity.

The equivalent additional draught beers to the above are:

60/-: Wm. Younger's XXP Newcastle IPA.

70/-:Wm. Younger's XXPS.

80/-: Wm. Younger's IPA and No 3 Scotch Ale, Newcastle Exhibition.

Wm. Younger's draught beers often go under the generic name of 'Scotch Ale'.

Keg   Tartan Bitter.

    Tartan Mild.

    Both of these are keg beers which are sold in England.

Tartan Special. The Scottish equivalent of Tartan bitter.

Newcastle Exhibition. The draught beer in keg form.

McEwan's Export. A slightly stronger keg beer.

McEwan's Pale Ale. A lighter keg beer.

Starbrite. Another lightish keg beer.

Harp Lager.

Bottled   McEwan's Pale.

    McEwan's Blue Label.

    McEwan's Export.

    McEwan's Strong.

These are pale ales in ascending order of strength.

Younger's Pale Ale.

Younger's Brown.

Younger's Stout.* A sweet stout.

Younger's Export. A strong pale ale.

Younger's No 3. A medium gravity darkish ale.

Younger's Double Century Ale. A strong dark ale.

Newcastle Amber. A pale ale from Tyneside.

Newcastle Strong Brown ale.* The well-known 'Newcastle Brown' which is a strong dark ale rather than a brown ale.

Harp Lager.*

Canned   The bottled beers marked * above are also in cans, as also is Younger's Tartan Special. In addition there is a 4 pint can of Tartan Special, and one of Starbrite called 'Newcastle Big Four'.

Draught beers are dispensed by all systems but mainly by top pressure CO_2.

WATNEY MANN LTD

REGISTERED OFFICE

Watney House, Palace Street, London SW1. Tel 01-834 1266.

FACTS AND FIGURES ABOUT THE GROUP

Watney Mann Ltd is a group with a wide spread of

activities and around 6,000 licensed houses spread over most of Britain, but thinnest in North Wales and the extreme north of England. There are eight operating breweries at present (not including the recent acquisition of Samuel Webster of Halifax) which will, by 1980, be concentrated at four centres—Edinburgh, Manchester, Norwich and London (Mortlake).

Watney Mann is now part of the Grand Metropolitan Hotels group.

Watney Mann was formed in 1958 as a result of a merger between Watney Combe Reid & Co Ltd and Mann, Crossman & Paulin Ltd, each with breweries in London.

International Distillers & Vintners Ltd recently became part of the Grand Metropolitan Hotels group and brought in a large Scotch whisky production of blended and malt whiskies, also gin (Gilbeys Gin), vodka (Smirnoff Vodka) and a range of table wines, sherries and ports.

Specialised retail companies within the group are Peter Dominic and Westminster Wine, retail wine and spirit merchants; Justerini & Brooks Ltd, wine merchants; Schooner Inns (40, and more on the way); steak/scampi houses; Buckingham Restaurants Ltd (15, and more planned); Watney Mann (Entertainments) Ltd with 13 (will be 50) discotheque/entertainment 'Birds Nest' houses; Watney Mann Hotels Ltd with 22 hotels; and Watney Lyon Motels Ltd with 9 motels and plans for a tenth.

Wholesale interests include Gilbey Vintners Ltd, Morgan Furze & Co Ltd (wine service to catering trade), and Coca-Cola Southern Bottlers. Associated companies are Carlsberg Brewery Ltd (Watney 49 per cent interest, Carlsberg of Copenhagen 51 per cent)—

a £12 million lager brewery at Northampton is being built; Cantrell & Cochrane Ltd, 'Club' mineral waters and fruit drinks; and Taunton Cider Co Ltd.

There are three breweries and some 4,500 retail outlets in Belgium and beers are brewed under licence in Spain and Italy. There are 600 outlets in France supplied by the Belgian breweries. In all, Watney Mann beers are available in 40 countries.

RECOGNITION

The house sign is to be seen over most of the country—a conspicuous red barrel on which is written 'Watneys' in white.

The recently acquired Samuel Webster & Sons Ltd of Halifax with just over 250 houses covering a large part of Yorkshire is recognised by predominantly green signs depicting a figure of 'Young Sam' and a barley sheaf over a pint mug.

BEERS

National

Draught & keg	Watneys Red. A well balanced keg beer with a burnt malty characteristic.
	Watneys Special Bitter. A medium bitter draught beer.
	Watneys Star Light. A lower cost, lighter bitter.
	Watneys Special Mild. A dark, sweet mild.
Bottled	Watneys Pale. A traditional pale ale.

Straight 8. A new 'special' pale beer in ½ pint bottles and 9⅔oz cans.

Export Gold (light).

Stingo (dark).

Both of these are barley wines.

Watneys Brown.

Manns Brown. A higher-gravity brown ale.

Both of these are medium sweet brown ales.

Take-home cans — Party Four and Party Seven. The Star Light in can.

The bottled beers are also available in cans.

Regional

Several local beers are brewed such as Norwich Bitter in East Anglia and Great Northern Bitter in the north of England (Wilson's of Manchester—checkerboard signs). Samuel Webster beers include Best Bitter and Pennine Bitter with characteristic flavours, a light and dark mild and a range of bottled beers. Drybrough in Edinburgh produce a range of keg and bottled beers for Scotland as follows.

Keg — Drybrough Keg Export.

Drybrough Keg Heavy.

Drybrough Keg Light.

These three are in order of strength (Export is the strongest) and have a characteristic nutty, malty flavour.

Bottled & cans — Starbright. A light ale.

Export Ale. Stronger than the Starbright.

Manns Special Brown Ale.

WHITBREAD & CO LTD

REGISTERED OFFICE

Brewery, Chiswell Street, London EC1. Tel 01-606-4455.

The Chiswell Street Brewery is of historic interest, dating from 1750 and retaining several eighteenth-century features.

A team of shire horses is kept by Whitbread & Co for shows and also for delivering beer in London's East End near the brewery.

FACTS AND FIGURES ABOUT THE GROUP

The group owns some 8-9,000 pubs and 1,000 off-licences, and an extensive free trade via many outlets including some regional brewers who distribute Whitbread national beers by arrangement.

There are 20 operating breweries—including one overseas—19 bottling plants, 10 mineral water factories, 40 distribution depots and 2 hop farms.

Companies and breweries within the group are as follows (note that the name of the original brewer is given, as some of their signs and names may still be on the houses).

Whitbread East Pennines Ltd. Brewing at Sheffield, Kirkstall and Leeds (Woodlesford—Bentley's Yorkshire Breweries—ceased brewing in 1972) and Castle Eden, Co Durham (Nimmo).

Whitbread West Pennines Ltd. Brewing at Blackburn (Duttons), Liverpool (Threlfalls) and Salford (Threlfalls Chesters). A new modern brewery opened at Samlesbury in 1972.

Whitbread Wales. Brewing at Cardiff and Rhymney.

Whitbread Flowers. Brewing at Cheltenham (Flowers and West Country Ales) and Tiverton ('Tivvy Ales'—ex Starkey, Knight & Ford).

Whitbread Fremlins. Brewing at Faversham (Fremlins) and Wateringbury.

Whitbread Wessex. Brewing at Romsey ('Strong Country') and Portsmouth (Brickwood—the sunshine sign). Ex Mew Langton houses in the Isle of Wight also form part of Whitbread Wessex.

Whitbread Wethereds. Brewing at Marlow on the Thames.

As well as Chiswell St there is the brewery at Luton.

RECOGNITION

The house sign can be seen in every county of the United Kingdom and beyond. This is a golden hind's head on a white tankard which is on a cherry red background framed in gold. Licensed houses frequently depict 'Whitbread' in white faced script also on a cherry red background and framed in gold. This may be adapted to fit the type of pub and surroundings and the cherry red signs are often a very conspicuous feature of the pub's outside walls. Pictorial signs often have the 'Whitbread' motif on a cherry red band above the painting.

BEERS

National

Draught   Whitbread Trophy Bitter. A draught

bitter which is produced at all the above breweries except Wateringbury. Not necessarily identical from one area to another.

Whitbread Best Mild. A dark mild.

Keg Whitbread Tankard. A keg beer which has an extensive distribution in free trade and clubs and also via some regional brewers by arrangement.

Heineken Draught Lager. Brewed at Luton under licence, the English version of the international Dutch lager.

Stella Artois. A high-gravity Belgian lager.

Bottled Whitbread Pale Ale.

Whitbread Light Ale. Of slightly lower gravity than the PA.

Brewmaster. A pale ale with 'a soft, smooth palate, somewhat similar to lager'.

Final Selection. A dark barley wine with a dry finish.

Gold Label. A light barley wine originated by Tennants of Sheffield of very high gravity—blended and matured. One of the strongest beers in the country.

Forest Brown. A dryish brown ale.

Poacher Brown. Another brown ale but a little sweeter.

Mackeson. A full-bodied sweet stout, widely available in the free trade. The name originates from Mackeson & Co Ltd, brewers of Hythe, Kent, which became wholly owned by the Whitbread group in the sixties.

	Whitbread Special Stout. Less sweet than Mackeson. Heineken Lager.
Canned	Whitbread Pale Ale and Light Ale, Mackeson, Forest Brown, Heineken Lager, Export (northern half of country only), Jumbo/Blue Can (4 pints/7 pints of bitter).
Non returnable bottles	Gold Label

Regional

Draught Trophy Bitter is brewed in each of the regions. Other regional beers include the following.

East Pennines

Draught & Keg	XXX, a draught mild; Brew 70, an experimental draught bitter of lower gravity than Trophy; Gauntlet, a strong keg bitter at present test-marketed in Kent, Hampshire, Sheffield and Leeds; Amber, a light mild.
Bottled	Trophy Pale Ale, in the north only; Export Pale Ale, in Castle Eden area only.
Canned	Export, north only.

West Pennines

Draught	B, a bitter from Duttons; BB, also from Duttons but of a higher gravity than B; Mild, a dark mild from Duttons; Amber, a light mild from Duttons and Threlfalls;

| | XXX, a strong mild; Chesters Best Mild, from Salford—a dark mild with a good following in the Manchester area. |
| Bottled | OBJ, a barley wine from Duttons. |

Wales

| Draught & Keg | BA, Best Ale. PMA, Pale Mild Ale. This is weaker in gravity and lighter than the BA; Starbright, a local keg beer. |
| Bottled | Ski Lager. |

Flowers

| Draught & Keg | Pale Ale and Special Pale Ale, both bitters brewed for a local following; Starbright, a local keg beer; XX, a mild. |
| Bottled | Tivvy, a brown ale. |

Fremlins

| Draught & Keg | Gauntlet, a strong keg beer as above; AK, a light mild; XX, a dark mild. |
| Bottled | County Ale, a strongish pale ale; Gold Top, 'Stock Ale'—a strong ale suited to diabetics (and also non-diabetics). |

Wessex

| Draught & Keg | Best Bitter, from Brickwoods; Gauntlet, in 'Strong Country'; AK, a sweetish mild; Mild, from Brickwoods. |
| Bottled | Sunshine, light ale from Brickwoods; Golden IPA, a pale ale from Strong of Romsey; Light Ale, from Brickwoods; Rumsey Brown a medium sweet brown |

ale from Strongs; Brown Ale, from Brickwoods.

Wethereds

Draught   IPA, a hoppy bitter with a good local following.

London area only

Draught   Best Bitter.

Many types of dispensing systems are in use.

CHAPTER 9

Postscript

If anyone is lucky enough to drink all (or even some) of the beers in this book he will surely be convinced that beer is a drink to be treated with great respect and discrimination. Many people enter a pub and call for a beer or bitter without specifying the brand—even when confronted with a gleaming variety of counter mountings or choice of casks from different sources such as might be encountered in a free house. Faced with real choice, in fact, many people are not quite sure what to order, with the result that they may receive the most unsuitable or merely the most expensive—the landlord has been left to make the decision, and he does not know the customer's preferences. The most expensive beer is not necessarily the best value for money or the beer that the customer would prefer.

It is to encourage the discriminating drinker that this book was compiled, and perhaps conversations such as took place between a dedicated beer-drinker called Acton and an 'oleaginous wine-waiter in a plushy [ie predatory] Sydney restaurant' will one day become commonplace: Acton is a fictitious character in the novel *Pantaloons and Antics* by the Australian author Cyril Pearl. He astonished this wine-waiter by asking for a beer-list and the dialogue went as follows.

'No wine', said Acton. 'But I'd like to have a look at the beer-list, please'.

'I beg your pardon, Sir?'

'Surely the biggest hotel in the biggest beer-drinking city in the world has a beer list?'

'I'm afraid not, Sir!'

'Incredible'. Acton shook his head sadly. 'Well, please ask the cellar-master if he has a bottle of '61 Foster's. It was a memorable year for Victorian beer, with that delicate flavour of bushfires in the hops. The '61 Foster's is a really superb lager, brut, mon, charnu, petillante, fino, pizzicato, and faintly amertume. It has that nobly fading straw-like pallor which is less a colour than a vestment, *la robe*: and an aroma that is distinctly Bouverie Street. The bouquet is a discreet cuir russe, or Old Harness. It is urbane but quietly persuasive, and with a notable wet finish, soft on the taste-buds, and on the pocket, too'.

The '61 Foster's was exhausted, but Acton found a tolerable '62 Melbourne Bitter to go with the coffee. He assured the wine-waiter that, though it lacked chiaroscuro and clangtint, it had a compensatory verve, good-humoured spritzig, and almost the panache of a pre-war Export Bass.

Readers who have lasted this far may be assured that beers with good-humoured spritzig can be found in every county of Britain.

Recent changes and additions (up to the end of May 1973)

The Carlisle and District State Management Scheme has been wound up and most of the pubs have been acquired by Greenall Whitley (48 pubs), Courage (John Smith) (27) and Scottish & Newcastle (26). Jennings of Cockermouth bought a number and about 30 of the smaller pubs were sold to tenants. The brewery was bought by a local businessman (Mr Peter Lewis) and his associates who intend, if possible, to continue brewing operations. This will depend on the result of a feasibility and economic study.

The entry of outsiders into the brewing industry has continued with the acquisition of *Dudgeon & Co Ltd.* The name of this company has been changed to Belhaven Brewery Co Ltd which now forms the Brewery and Inns Division of Clydesdale Commonwealth Hotels (Investments). There has been no alteration in the brewing policy but the original seven outlets have been increased by an additional 16 hotels which are expected to become 50 by the end of 1973. Also, *The Hull Brewery* is now a member of Northern Foods but remains an independent brewing company. *The Workington Brewery* has been taken over by Mount Charlotte Investments. This firm also made bids for *Jennings Brothers* in order to merge the two breweries and close down Jennings. A bitter takeover battle to save the Cockermouth brewery resulted in victory for Jennings, which therefore remains independent.

Adnams of Southwold have developed a flourishing free trade and their beers may now be found well outside the trading area as follows: White Horse, Kersey; White Horse, Hadleigh; Bull, Thorpe Morieux; Angel Hotel, Bury St Edmunds; Bell, Clare; Crown, Long Melford; Rose Inn, Stoke-by-Nayland; Blue Boar, Maldon; Victory, Wickham St Pauls; Drapers House restaurant, Earls Colne. In the Cambridge area at the Queens Head, Newton; Tickell Arms, Whittlesford; Golden Ball, Boxworth. Two recently acquired pubs are the Six Bells, Gislingham, and the British Grenadier, Colchester. Adnams draught bitter may be found in some Whitbread pubs in Norfolk and Suffolk by virtue of a trading agreement. Adnams' Fisherman Strong has been re-named Fisherman Brown.

Melbourns Brewery have acquired the residential Crown Hotel in Stamford. Their keg bitter has been re-named Crest.

Vaux Breweries have taken over *Ward & Co* of Sheffield. It is understood that although Ward's bottled beers will be phased out, Ward's agreeable draught beers will still be brewed.

A new brewhouse and bottling line has been opened at *Samuel Webster's* brewery in Halifax. Webster was taken over by Watney Mann in 1972 and is now part of the Grand Metropolitan Hotels group. It now seems likely that Webster's distinctively flavoured beers should continue to be available in their 250-300 pubs in Halifax and the surrounding area.

Shepherd Neame have adopted 'Master Brew' as a generic name for their draught Bitter, Mild and Ale.

A new beer has been introduced by *Gale & Co* called 'Treble Seven' which is a keg dark mild with an OG of 1034. There are now 90 pubs owned by Gale and they include The Four Horseshoes at Long Sutton near Odiham, and the Black Lion at Woodcote which makes four in all to the north of Reading.

With the opening of their new plant at Runcorn, *Bass Charrington* are closing a number of breweries in the North West.

Young & Co of Wandsworth have acquired the East India Arms in Fenchurch Street, London EC3. Two more Young pubs are due to open in 1973—the Catford Ram in Catford, and the Champion in Merton Road, SW19.

A battle over beer is brewing up in the EEC. West Germany fears that plans to standardise Europe's brewing laws may lower its high standards. A law dating from 1516 requires only malted barley, hops, yeast and water to be used in brewing bottom-fermented beers. This law applies also to top-fermented beers in some areas. The Community Commission wish to allow beer to contain up to thirty per cent of either rice, maize, potato starch, millet or manioc. Britain, where sugar and cereals other than barley are permitted (excepting the Isle of Man), may find itself on the opposite side in this dispute.

In general, more and more keg beers, bright beers and pressurised draught beers are being sold in some areas—a trend towards gassy beer with less character and flavour which is fostered by some of the industry. Pressurised draught beers can be especially gassy because there are two sources of CO_2 —the beer's own, and that from the dispensing cylinder. Predictions have been made that the incidence of ulcers may increase because of acidity in the stomach (CO_2 forms carbonic acid in water). Fears have recently been expressed that colourful pub signs may disappear and be replaced more and more by standard brewery advertisements. There have been many pubs sold, either as private dwellings or as free houses. Many of these appear to be more concerned with providing good food than good beer. They may also be 'tied' to a certain brewer who has financed alterations or decorations. It is also difficult for a free house to offer a good choice of regional beers if there are no breweries within reasonable delivery distance.

However, small brewers continue to supply a wide range of specialised products for their local specialised markets—the kind of products which the major national groups find it uneconomic to produce. There is a clear need in the industry for the· small independent brewer and the *Morning Advertiser,* the trade paper of the Licensed Victuallers, commented on the threatened closure of Barnsley Brewery in its leading article of 22 February 1973 as follows: 'Rationalisation in the Brewing Industry has gone far enough . . . local prides and local brews have been eliminated with cold disregard for the feelings of licensees or customers . . .' This is a sentiment with which many people would agree, and the paper went on to say that in ten years' time there would be heard remarks like 'Y' should ha' tasted t'owd Barnsley beer, lad. Now that were beer . . .'

FROM MAY 1973 to FEBRUARY 1974

Gray & Sons Ltd is due to cease production in

September 1974. The brewery has been sold to meet heavy estate duties arising from the death of Mr Gray's father. The firm will remain independent and distribute various beers (at present, Ridley's bottled beers) from a depot at Galleywood. A decision about supply of draught beers may be made by June. *Selby Brewery* has acquired its first pub, the Board Inn at Howden. CAMRA (207 Keats Court, Salford 7, Lancs. See p. 70) has mushroomed into an important organisation to protect the consumer. Membership has risen to over 10,000 and increasing daily. Its *Good Beer Guide* is due for publication by John Waddington Ltd in March 1974. *The Carlisle brewery* was sold to a firm not connected with brewing, the deal with Mr Lewis having fallen through for mysterious reasons. The future of the brewery is now uncertain.

Tenant's associations have been formed, and the help of MPs sought, to fight the large brewers' policies of replacing tenants by managers. Some of the most successful tenants have been given notice—penalised by success. The Liberal Party has reaffirmed its support for the national 'Save the Tenant' campaign. The Liberals are 'gravely worried at the growth of monopoly in the brewing industry, the decline in the quality of the product and the steady increase in price'. They are also protesting against other abuses by the large combines.

The Blackpool brewery of Bass Charrington and the Rochdale brewery of Samuel Smith are due for imminent closure. The Trowbridge, Wilts brewery of Watney Mann will continue production. Whitbread plans to close its Chiswell Street brewery which may mean that draught beer will not be available in Whitbread pubs in London, only 'processed' beer.

Whitbread are changing to top pressure beers in many pubs, and also closing many pubs—unfortunately followed by much of the industry, especially the nationals. Their policy of centralising production seems strange in view of the fuel crisis, transport costs, and frequent strikes (causing beer shortages) at the large production centres.

New beers include Heritage to replace Matthew Brown's existing keg beer (Lion Stout has been replaced by Mackeson); a strong 'Centenary Ale' from J.W. Cameron; Hi-Brau lager from Guernsey Brewery Co; Mitre strong pale ale from McMullens; North Country in keg, bottles and cans from Hull Brewery; '1073' strong ale from Northern Clubs'; Conquest to replace Tollykeg, and '250', a strong ale from Tolly Cobbold. *Belhaven Brewery* has increased its outlets, via CCH Investments' hotels, to more than 200. *Boddingtons'* now has 10 pubs in St Helens—exchanged with Greenall Whitley. *Everards Brewery* has acquired pubs in Nottingham and nearby in a deal with Whitbread (the Vernon; Golden Fleece, Upper Broughton; Crown, Shepshed), also 2 Courage pubs in Northampton. *Higsons Brewery* has sold its pubs in Leek and the Potteries to Wolverhampton & Dudley Breweries. The last outpost to the south east is now the Fool's Nook just south of Macclesfield. Processed beer (chilled and filtered) is gradually replacing draught beer in some instances. *John Peel* ales (Workington Brewery) are now in Mount Charlotte Investments' hotels in the south west (eg in Cheltenham, Bristol, Exeter, Paignton, Bude and Cardiff). *Rayment & Co's* bottled beers except for Pelham Ale have been discontinued.

Index of Brewers